Praise for PT

"I distinctly remember a time when Pastor Tim and I served together. We ended up praying for seniors in high school at their last official student camp before they went off to college. Pastor Tim and I sensed that whole weekend they were struggling to open up to the priceless love of God. Right before they were coming in to be prayed for, I had spent time with them. They shared some of the areas they were struggling with. It was stopping them from truly worshiping and they needed a release from their past sins and guilt. As they came into the prayer room to be prayed for, it was one of the most powerful experiences I have ever seen. Pastor Tim, as he was praying what he was hearing from the Lord, prayed over all their struggles. I could literally see the burden and shame lifted off. Praise God! When you know how God feels about you, which is unchanging, it is a catalyst to experience freeing worship and to go into a great adventure with Jesus."

~Pastor Paul Kim, *Seattle New Life Lead Pastor, Seattle, Washington*

"The thing in my life that I consider most valuable above all else is the intimacy I have with Jesus. Hearing his voice and being close to Him is something I treasure beyond words. I am forever grateful to Pastor Tim for taking the time to mentor me so that I could grow in hearing God's voice. If you desire to know God more intimately and follow him more obediently, this book is a lifetime of wisdom poured out on how to be a radical follower of Jesus Christ."

~Julie Futch, *Nurse and Worship Leader, Lexington, Kentucky*

"Personally witnessing Tim Jones' transformation by the power of the Holy Spirit for over 33 years, I've been the beneficiary of many listening prayers which met me and others SPOT ON! He has modeled a way of life—listening to, and following Jesus by hearing and obeying God's voice—no matter what the cost, for which I will ever be grateful."

*~**Pastor Ginger Holland**, Cornerstone United Methodist, Tupelo, Mississippi*

"Listening to the voice of the Lord is such a foundational teaching for this generation, yet is rarely taught within the Body of Christ. For a few years, I have watched Pastor Tim follow the voice of God and I am amazed at the fruit and power that this simple act of listening and obeying what God says has produced fruit in his life and in others, especially for young adults. I have been deeply encouraged and touched by Pastor Tim's ministry, and believe He has something that could awaken this generation to the exiting adventure of loving, and following Jesus. As Samuel was raised up on a time where hearing the voice of the Lord was rare, I believe Pastor Tim has been raised up at this hour to help train this young generation on hearing God's voice, and restore this lost doctrine for the Body of Christ."

*~**José Baeza, Director,** Awaken Love Ministries, Georgetown College*

"Pastor Tim got in prayer to start a campus prayer ministry here at EKU. As soon as I heard his idea, I jumped on board. Through a small group of 15-20 other students God has invaded this campus and is changing the hearts of everyone that comes to our weekly bible study. Our focus is to have an unrelenting hunger for God and be His mouthpiece, and we know God will do the rest. Listening prayer has brought many of us into a closer and more meaningful relationship with God. I encourage anyone reading this book to seek after God's voice with everything they have. Hearing God's voice and following Jesus through listening prayer will be the greatest adventure you will ever be a part of. Are you ready for the thrill of your life?!?!"

*~**Travis Rose**, Student-Athlete (Golf team) and Senior at Eastern Kentucky University*

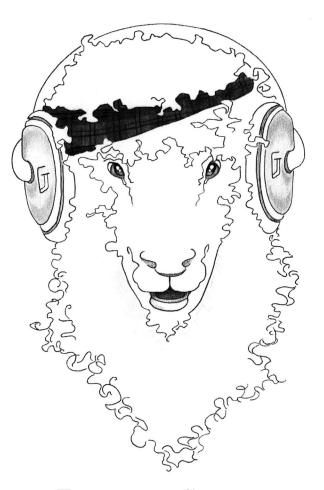

EXTREME SHEEP

Experiencing Listening Prayer

Pastor Tim Jones

SCROLLS OF ZEBULON
A PUBLISHING COMPANY

Scrolls of Zebulon
Mobile, AL USA

Extreme Sheep: Experiencing Listening Prayer
©2017 by Timothy Jones

For inquiries, contact:
Scrolls of Zebulon Publishing
P.O. Box 190309
Mobile, AL USA 36619-0939
www.scrollsofzebulon.com — info@scrollsofzebulon.com

"Extreme Sheep" original character artwork by Ember Kawarada
Photo of Timothy Jones by Ashley McKinney Brown

Cover and Interior Design by Sarah Smith
Edited by Rachel L. Hall

ISBN: 978-09982135-6-9 (SC)

Library of Congress: 2017904249

Printed in the United States

This book is dedicated to Brother Harold Kastner, my spiritual mentor and Father in the faith. Brother Harold faithfully modeled for me what it looks like to follow Jesus through listening to His voice in prayer. Brother Harold's consecrated life continues to serve as an inspiration to me each and every day of my life. Brother Harold is now a part of that great cloud of witnesses that is cheering us on to carry out our daily assignments for the sake of the Kingdom of God!

TABLE OF CONTENTS

Acknowledgments

First, I'd like to thank the Lord Jesus Christ for saving me and giving me the incredible honor of serving Him. I can't say thank you enough to the Lord for being so patient with me and giving me the opportunity to say yes to the Holy Spirit through listening prayer.

I'd like to thank Rachel Hall for her guidance and for the wonderful job of editing for this book.

I'd like to thank Ember Kawarada for her original drawing of the Extreme Sheep on the book cover.

Thank you to Ashley McKinney Brown for the Extreme Sheep photography.

Thanks to all the people that submitted listening prayer stories for the book that have been so helpful in telling the story of listening prayer.

Finally, thanks to our Campus Thirst and Experiencing Listening Prayer ministry team. Our hope and prayer is that this book will help activate people into the joy of following Jesus through listening prayer!

FOREWORD

From a Pastor

"Have you met Pastor Tim?" That question was asked of me countless times over the years whenever I would drive an hour from my house to a little prayer barn outpost outside of Louisville, Kentucky. They would say, "You come all the way here from Lexington, hungry for God, I am shocked that you have never met Pastor Tim Jones—he lives in your city and always hangs out at the coffee shop." I thought, "No way, I always hang out there— how have I not met the man they say hears incredibly from God?" So, I began to pray, "Father if you desire for me to meet Pastor Tim would you connect our paths?"

One week later I was eating breakfast with a friend when he mentioned his close friend Pastor Tim… my antennae immediately went up and I said, "Could you introduce us?" The next week I get a call and my friend says, "Come to my house, PT (as he is affectionately known) is here." I hopped in the car, broke a few traffic laws, and got to his house as soon as possible. There I met the man that there was no mistaking; this man could hear the voice of the Father!

I had always been skeptical of listening prayer in the past. People joke, "Prayer is when you talk to God, schizophrenia is when God talks to you!" But I sat there speechless; jaw on the floor, thinking, "Wha? Wha? What was that?" As Pastor Tim prayed for me, the secrets of my heart were completely revealed! There was just no mistaking it, He could hear so clearly.

We serve a talking God. Jesus said, "My sheep know my voice." Do you really believe that? Why do so many Christians today operate as though God has lost His voice; like for the past two thousand years He has had a bad case of divine laryngitis? In this incredibly practical book, my mentor and friend, Pastor Tim Jones, talks openly about how to grow in listening and hearing the voice of the Father. You will be amazed at the journey that God is about to take you on through the pages of this book and then into your daily life. You will see maximum impact like you never thought possible as you apply to your life what Pastor Tim Jones teaches. I am excited for the body of Christ all over the earth when they begin getting activated into hearing the voice of the Father.

Cameron McDonald, *Lead Pastor, SoAcres Church*
Lexington, Kentucky

From a Student

I was a freshman at a weekend retreat with a university ministry. It was late at night, maybe 11:00 p.m. The main building was a madhouse due to a very intense water gun fight occurring between hundreds of students. The main building held the common room, prayer room, and snacks. At the time, everyone was either gathered for food, fighting, or prayer. A strange mix! Even more strange, in the middle of the war was a long line of students waiting outside the prayer room. Some had been waiting so long to go in and be prayed for by some guy that they were seated along the wall and laughing as people got soaked and lost the war.

After having received prayer, some students came out of the room simultaneously sobbing with relief and laughing without explanation: "It's like he knows everything about me!" Others came out with dropped jaws, blank faces, and quickly left the building: "I have no idea what just happened." Other students were unfazed: "God spoke to me! It was awesome! You gotta go in and get prayed for!"

And there I was, petrified and thinking to myself, "Freaks." At the time, I thought I was scared of the man they called PT, short for Pastor Tim. PT is an old guy. He has white hair and wears running shoes wherever he goes. He always wears plaid (always, unless he's officiating a wedding). He's the only old guy I know of who can work an iPhone without assistance. He can walk and text. His phone and laptop have fake Bible covers over them. Oh, and we can't forget that he knows everything about you.

He's a freak. And I decided I didn't want anything to do with this guy. Whoever he was.

Over the course of the next year I couldn't get rid of him. He was everywhere. My sister and all my friends had been "prayed" for by him. He was always showing up to various ministries and churches I was attending. Everyone talked about him and his gift of prayer and prophecy. I ran into him on campus, at the coffee shop, everywhere. I turned around and avoided eye contact.

I specifically remember him sitting at a table near me at the coffee shop, sometime around my freshman year. I watched him sit down wearing another plaid shirt and pull out his Bible covered laptop and phone. I watched students come up to him and ask to be prayed for. They were all so giddy and weird. "Something is wrong with them," I thought. I left soon after.

As I left I heard God speak to my heart, "You're not afraid of him and his voice."

I had spent that summer doing mission work in Costa Rica. And the entire time God was revealing to me that I fear God's voice; I block God out because I'm afraid of what He will say or do. It was a fear I had carried since I was a child. There was no reason or source, it was simply a fear I had. A misunderstanding of who God is.

"You're afraid of My voice."

And it hit me. The truth. I was so afraid of God condemning me. At the same time, I was also afraid of Him telling me about a wonderful and beautiful future. I was simultaneously so afraid of being in trouble for not stepping up to the plate as I was of hearing "Well done, my child," and being called deeper and further into God's plan. Simply, I was afraid. So God began putting in my heart a desire to allow His voice both in my heart and through the prayers of other people.

That very semester a good friend of mine began hosting a monthly worship night at his house. Sometimes over 100 students came. Predictably, I heard PT would be there. With reluctance, I walked into the house. It was full of freaks.

"Oh God, don't make me do this!" I begged.

"Do not fear My voice," I heard back.

As an introvert, this was already my worst nightmare. The entire house was full of people. Weird people. People singing, praying, dancing. People talking about the goodness of God when I wasn't quite convinced He was all that good.

PT was seated on the couch in the living room. "Now or never," I thought and gutted up to meet the guy I thought was off-the-charts weird.

"Well, hello," he began.

He thought I was my sister who had already been prayed for—we're twins.

"Hey, I haven't actually met you. I'm Rhea's twin," I explained.

"OH!"

"And I'm just going to tell you that I don't actually want to be prayed for. But I feel like God wants me to. So, here I am."

"Okay, well I'm just going to pray for you with listening prayer. Alright?"

I was so nervous, looking for any reason to escape, "Okay...."

But he began too quickly: "I plead the blood of Jesus over

this time of prayer and in the name of Jesus I command that only the Holy Spirit shall come close and prosper."

And my thoughts ran wild, "Okay, so he gives credit that it's the Holy Spirit who is speaking. I guess that's legit."

He continued, "God loves you so much. Thank you, Lord, that Cara has a heart for the hopeless, abandoned, and broken. Thank you, Lord, that she has an evangelistic call on her life."

Okay, well, that's true... Probably a good guess.

"Thank you, Lord, that you want Cara to know that her future will be good, it will be positive..."

It's like he knows I'm scared that my future is going to be bad and I'm not sure God is good...

"Lord, she has had a really hard past." His eyes twinkled as they looked in mine, and he spoke softly. "Thank you Lord that you see how discouraged and crushed Cara feels. Lord, you know that she has a hurt heart and thinks that no one can heal it. Thank you, Lord, that you *can* heal it."

No, there are parts that will always hurt.

"Thank you, Lord, that even the parts that you don't think anyone can ever heal, you will heal."

Okay, this is getting weird.

"Thank you Lord that you are breaking off any fear or worry of the future, thank you, Lord, that you are going to walk with Cara. Thank you that you want her to know that you are real, and not a figment of her imagination."

Oh, my gosh. He knows I doubt that God is actually in my heart and mind, he knows I'm questioning if God is real.

"Lord, you see how Cara has questions and that she is you a logical thinker. Thank you, Lord, that Cara doesn't have to be so hard on herself. Thank you, Lord, that she is going to be a teacher and discipler. Thank you, Lord, that she is going to be able to help people, especially nonbelievers, process their faith."

My mind was blown. Whatever else he said as he closed was drowned out by my racing thoughts. He's never met me; he knows nothing about me. Yet he's pulling out things from the most hidden parts of my heart and restoring in me the calling and purpose I have hoped that God is forming through my hard past and skepticism.

"What is this?" I asked myself.

As time went on, I still felt intimidated. Anytime I saw PT or heard he was around I tended to keep a distance; I was still battling skepticism and fear. One day I was at work: I was a college student managing at a frozen yogurt shop. Doesn't get more hipster than that. There hadn't been a single customer in the store for a while when I heard the doorbell chime. I walked up front to greet the customer, "Hi, welcome to— Wait, I know you."

There he was. The white-haired fellow in plaid. In my store. Just the two of us. Sigh.

I felt awkward standing there behind the counter so I walked around to hug him. It was in his hesitant expression that I realized I knew him, but he didn't remember me. Must be an old guy bad memory thing.

"I'm Cara. You prayed for me at the Nightwatch event like two months ago."

"Oh yes, how are you?"

We got to talking (I was still upset he was in my store, alone, and I had nowhere to run or hide!) when he told me, "I was on a prayer drive and the Lord led me here to pray for someone."

"A prayer drive?" I asked.

"Yea. Some days the Lord leads me to go on a prayer drive. As I'm listening in prayer, I receive 'left' and 'right' until I end up somewhere and I'm supposed to go in and pray for someone."

Ugh. As if he couldn't get any weirder.

I looked around the store and said, "Well, I'm the only one here." And I knew what that meant.

"That's awesome! Can I pray for you?"

Somehow, I couldn't say no, and God was still working in my heart to allow his voice through the prayers of other people. "Sure," I said and ushered him to a table.

"Okay. Cara, right?"

"Yes." It was strange to me that he didn't remember my name. He didn't even remember praying for me. I wasn't surprised. He probably has an old man's memory and was praying for as many as 100 students that night. It actually gave me relief that he didn't remember the details of my past. Or my heart and life. I was glad he had forgotten all about me.

"I plead the blood of Jesus over this time of prayer and in the name of Jesus I command that only the Holy Spirit shall close and prosper. Cara, God loves you. And he is so proud of you. Thank you, Lord, that Cara's future will be positive, and that she won't walk alone."

With this again? How did he know I was STILL struggling with this? Yet he forgot my name, let alone the last prayer he prayed over me.

"Thank you, Lord, that you already have someone special picked out for Cara."

That very summer I had broken up with my serious boyfriend and fell in love with someone else a month later. Then that guy broke my heart. At the time, I gave up on the idea of marriage. I just concluded there was no one on planet earth for me.

Even weirder though, that very summer a pastor in Costa Rica with the same gift of prayer told me the same thing. He told me to start praying for my husband because God had someone picked out for me. Could this be just a coincidence?

"Thank you, Lord, that Cara is going to be an amazing mother."

WHAT! I hate kids. And I'm terrified to raise another human being. There's no way that will ever happen.

"Lord, you see how Cara feels dislocated, like she has two homes. She's in one place but her heart is in another. Thank you, Lord, that you are strengthening her emotions, and that she won't feel jerked around from one place to another. Thank you that she will find contentment and understanding."

My heart fell, like a wall had been shattered and suddenly

there was hope. I do feel like that. Every night when I go to bed I'm so scared that my heart is always going to be split between two places. I'm so scared I will never feel a sense of placement or belonging.

"Thank you Lord that you are reminding her that you love her and of the enormity of the call on her life."

No, not me.

Eventually PT came to remember my name. And quickly he became a good friend and mentor. With every visit and prayer, I could feel God unraveling the skepticism in my heart. I could feel him tearing down my walls. Soon enough I was all in. God had met me in a place of darkness and spoke to the most hidden parts of my heart, places that inhibited him from working in me. I knew his voice and I no longer feared it.

Most importantly, I knew the Holy Spirit could speak to me through other people. And I desired more of it. I learned that my fear was never about Pastor Tim. It was never about what Pastor Tim said to me. Never about his gift or words of knowledge. My fear was of God's voice and his realness.

Lastly, I remember how I felt watching students at the retreat jaw-drop over PT and his freaky knowledge. Eventually, I saw it all with new eyes. This wasn't about him at all. It was about the close walk with God that allowed the Holy Spirit within a stranger to speak directly to the deepest part of another stranger's heart. It was about what God said. It was about what God did. This was about God. He was speaking through strangers to let me know that He is real, He loves me, and He knows the deepest parts of my heart. Not only is He real within my heart and mind, He is real within others as well.

This is what it is all about. Suddenly, as the last wall of my heart came tumbling down, I was all in. I wanted everyone to experience God like I did.

Cara Starns, *International Studies graduate, University of Kentucky, class of 2013*

EXTREME SHEEP
Experiencing Listening Prayer

Pastor Tim Jones

INTRODUCTION

There is nothing quite like going on a university campus and praying for students right there, out in the open, on the public sidewalks. When participants in Campus Thirst ministry teams pray, our desire is to pray straight from the heart of Jesus. We are learning to hear Jesus' voice in prayer. We have learned to get out of the way so that Jesus, the Good Shepherd, can minister to the heart of the person being prayed for. We call this type of prayer listening prayer. Through listening prayer people get a glimpse of who God created them to become should they say yes to Jesus. Typically, when people receive listening prayer, they are beyond intrigued by what has just happened to them. The Holy Spirit loves to impact people at a deep heart level to show them how real Jesus is. The Campus Thirst team does listening prayer to give those receiving the prayers experiences like the woman at the well had when she discovered that Jesus was the Son of God (John 4). We want everyone to experience what it is like to know and follow Jesus. So, this book is an invitation to you to become an extreme sheep—not like sheep who blindly follow every whim of modern culture, but like the sheep God names in scripture. Those like David, who called the Lord his shepherd; those who acknowledge Him and are called God's people (Psalm

100:3), those who follow because they know the voice of the Shepherd (John 10:27-28); those for whom Jesus sacrificed his life (John 10:15); and those to whom the King has given the inheritance of the Kingdom (Matt. 25:33). An extreme sheep is a powerful being that knows that his or her power and ability come from their shepherd rather than from any power or ability that they possess. Extreme sheep pay careful attention to the voice of their Good Shepherd because they know that following His voice is the key to their success.

After experiencing the joy of outreach prayer ministry on campus one day, I went to a coffee shop to begin to work on this book. A couple of months earlier, someone had sent a powerful recorded prayer that highlighted the importance of me not putting off an important writing assignment from the Lord. I had been receiving in prayer for years that I would write a book on listening prayer and so when this prayer showed up on in my voicemail, I thought, "Well, it's time!" The recorded prayer lit a fire in me since it dramatically confirmed that this writing assignment was from the Lord.

From the road, I began to write. After a few weeks of working on this book, I was writing in a coffee shop in Flagstaff, Arizona. I hopped up to get an ice water and an iced coffee. With a drink in each hand, I started back toward my seat. As I was trying to quickly step back so that a lady could pass by, I tripped over a little kid's booster seat and completely spilled one of my drinks. Thankfully, I barely recovered—just enough to not completely take out like a bowling ball a family of four sitting at a table. An awesome barista jumped in to help me clean up the mess. Everyone was trying hard to protect me from being embarrassed. Trust me, I wasn't embarrassed: I was excited! Why was I excited, you ask? I saw that my failed attempt at chivalry was opening the door to sharing with someone how much Jesus loved her. I ran out the door after the lady and told her that Jesus loved her so much. I could see that this message really touched her, aside from the fact that she was still in "Bless your little old heart" mode. When we realize how much Jesus really does love us, it literally changes every situation of life that we go through.

Months later I was in another coffee shop in Lexington, Kentucky. I was getting ready to work on this introduction having realized that the previous story indeed belonged in the introductory comments to assure you that this book is legit (obviously, I'm not cool enough to say *legit* but pretend that I am–just humor me). A friend walked up and introduced me to a student he wanted me to pray for. It turned out to be an amazing interruption from the Lord. After I prayed for the student, my friend surprised me and asked me to share why I believe in Jesus–in about four minutes. What would you say to this question? My first comment was, "Wow!" Then I jumped right in.

I shared that I was first attracted to Jesus because of His love for people. Jesus was willing to touch lepers, He reached out to the rejected, and He was willing to die on the cross for us. I also shared that I had been impressed by the love of the people that were representing Jesus to me. I shared with the student that I had decided in college that I wanted to be a famous actor (actually, I was shooting for being a second-rate actor–it's important to be realistic while you are being idealistic) and so I went on a Broadway tour sponsored by my college. However, what I saw in New York looked incredibly empty to me and not worth making the purpose of my life. Over the next couple of months, I decided to revisit what living for Jesus might look like. I started reading the Gospel of John in the New Testament but was confused about the miracles that Jesus did. I found Jesus raising Lazarus from the dead in John 11 to be particularly troubling. Much to my surprise, I found out that many of Jesus' miracles recorded in the New Testament are still happening today in Jesus' name. I told this student that I had discovered a purpose worth living for through following Jesus and that I do listening prayer for folks now to show them what an amazing relationship that they can have with Jesus as their Lord (leader) and Savior (forgiver of our sins). My friend and the student thanked me. I could see curiosity kicking in with the student I had prayed for, which is a good thing.

So why do I share all this? My hope is that this book will help you to believe that Jesus is the Son of God and to follow Him by listening to His voice. I also hope that you will be inspired to help others to believe in Jesus, too. It is a miracle that the creator of the universe wants to know us. Even after having been involved in listening prayer for eighteen years, I still can't wrap my mind around the way that the Lord loves us and wants to communicate with us in such a personal manner through listening prayer. That Jesus died on the cross to make this personal relationship possible is beyond my comprehension. When I first encountered listening prayer, I had no problem believing that God communicated with people in this way; I just had a hard time believing that I could ever know the Lord like this. I assumed that hearing from God so specifically was for special people—and, by the way, I was not special. Here is the astonishing truth: God loves to communicate in incredibly personal ways with ordinary people. Intimacy with Jesus and following Jesus is what listening prayer is all about, plain and simple!

The following prayer of Jesus' is the foundation of everything we do in listening prayer. We listen in prayer through Jesus, the Son of God, and our desire is to give glory to Jesus and to God the Father:

> After saying all these things, Jesus looked up to heaven and said, "Father, the hour has come. Glorify your Son so he can give glory back to you. For you have given him authority over everyone. He gives eternal life to each one you have given him. And this is the way to have eternal life—to know you, the only true God, and Jesus Christ, the one you sent to earth. I brought glory to you here on earth by completing the work you gave me to do. Now, Father, bring me into

the glory we shared before the world began." (John 17:1-5 NLT)

One evening while training college students hungry to move into listening prayer, Julie asked if she could pray for me as people were beginning to move about to pray for each other. During Julie's prayer for me, Jesus went to a place of tremendous disappointment in my life. Julie said, "Jesus wants you to know that you are finally going to hit a home run." Julie said she saw a picture of me standing on second base. This made me cry. When I was 12 years old, I went with my dad to visit a man from church who was hooked up to all kinds of tubes. He was incredibly sick. My dad promised him that I was going to hit a home run for him that day. My 12-year-old self felt the most incredible sense of responsibility. I had read the story about how Babe Ruth had promised a kid who was really sick that he was going to hit a home run for him and then Babe Ruth did just that. The legend was that he stepped out of the batter's box, pointed to the right field wall with his bat, and then hit a home run. To say that I was worked up is an understatement. To make matters worse, I had never hit a home run in my life.

For my first time at bat that day, I hit a ball that the center fielder caught just before it went over the wall. The friend of mine who caught the ball told me later that it was on its way out. My second time up, I grounded out. My last time at bat, I came up with two outs in the last inning. I kept fouling balls off. Finally, with a 3–2 count, I stepped out of the batter's box crying and mad. I pointed my bat toward the right center field wall just like Babe Ruth had done and held that bat suspended in the air for a while so that everyone who knew the story would know exactly what I was doing. Finally, I got back in the batter's box and *crack*: I got all of the ball! As I ran toward first base, I saw the ball bounce off the top of the wall, exactly where I had pointed. I was barely able to slide under the tag at second base. I stood on second base in the midst of the most incredible, crushing disappointment. I felt like I had let that poor, sick man down and that I had failed. And now, Jesus was saying that I was finally going to hit a home run. So I prayed, Lord, what does this mean? As I prayed into this over time, I realized that hitting a home run was for my personal glory. Now, my life was to be about living for Jesus' glory. I shared this emotional story with a college group I was helping to move into listening prayer. Ted, from that group, gave me one of his prized possessions: a Babe Ruth baseball card. Listening prayer is not about us; it's about Jesus. I have learned that helping people move into the joy of learning to follow Jesus through listening prayer is way better than hitting a home run!

While making finishing touches on this book, I took a quick trip to South Carolina so that I could pray for students all day in a coffeehouse and lead a group of students into experiencing listening prayer. During my trip, Tonya and Charlie introduced me to Barbara, who is 88. Barbara was about to retire to her room to spend some time with Jesus, but before she did, she told me a story about Joe. Barbara and Joe were married for over sixty years but they almost didn't meet. Joe was the youngest of ten children, and when Joe was two years old he was playing with his sisters. After a while, it was time for his sisters to bring the cows in to milk them. What Joe's sisters didn't know was that Joe attempted to trail after them. Joe got lost and he didn't even have a jacket. The nights got pretty cold in Ohio at that time of the year, and the whole family and neighbors were out searching for Joe all night. Finally, in the morning they had begun to drag the river, looking for Joe's body. Joe's brother found one of Joe's shoes about five miles away and continued to look for him from there. Suddenly Joe's brother spotted Joe's blond hair in the middle of a whole bunch of sheep. Joe had fallen asleep on the ground and the sheep and the lambs had all gathered around him to keep him warm. Imagine how surprised Joe's mom was, praying and crying in the kitchen, when her husband walked in holding Joe. Because of the sheep, Joe had nothing wrong with him. Before Joe fell asleep, he had climbed five barbed wire fences trying to find his way home when the sheep saved him. Tonya said that Barbara had the privilege of seeing Joe saved by a lamb for a second time when Jesus, the Lamb of God, took away Joe's sin. I told Barbara that I was turning in an edited copy of the manuscript of my book in a couple of days and that the name of the book was *Extreme Sheep*. Come on, you can't make this up!

So, hey, why not go for it: why not point your bat at the right field wall and hit some home runs for Jesus! The stories included here will encourage you to dare to listen to the voice of Jesus. He wants to take you on the greatest adventure you could ever have. His love for you is boundless. He is the Great Shepherd who leads His sheep. Trust me, if someone like me can learn to hear His voice, you can, too. Intrigued? Get ready for adventure. Why not get ready to become an extreme sheep!

CHAPTER 1

SURPRISED BY GOD

So, what do you do when you feel like you are living far below the kind of experiences with God that people in the Bible seemed to have? What do you do when you see prayer so highly valued by the people who are written about in the Bible, when your own experience with prayer is empty and seemingly devoid of meaning and power? What do you do as a pastor when people ask you to pray for them at important crossroads in their lives, and you feel ill-equipped to pray in any kind of significant way? What do you do when you feel as if you should know a whole lot more about something as important as prayer, and yet you are strangely silent about it from the pulpit?

In the beautiful mountains of North Carolina, I was preparing to preach a commitment service on the final night at a week-long youth retreat. In desperation, I asked a group of leaders to pray for me before the service started. Much to my surprise, spiritual power started going through me as these leaders prayed for me. One man put his hand on my head and something like electricity went through me. I had preached the message I was about to preach before, but I never experienced anything like what happened when I spoke that night. At the end of the message, I found myself saying, "If you would like to commit your life to the Lord Jesus Christ, come on the stage and face everyone in the auditorium." I honestly was shocked at what happened next. It sounded like canon fire as students left their auditorium seats and headed toward the stage. Suddenly, one of the boys went straight for the microphone. I thought, "I had better head that kid off because I don't know what he is going to say." The next thing I knew, I had lost my way to the microphone. The youth was now at the microphone, and I was thinking, "I thought I was going to stop that guy!" He said, "I commit my life to the Lord Jesus Christ." The next thing I knew, every kid on that platform walked over to the microphone and said, "I commit my life to the Lord Jesus Christ." I stood over by the piano weeping and was forever changed. The Lord put a hunger in my heart to know Him that night through listening prayer, even though at the time I had no clue that was what He was doing.

For the Apostle Paul, living in the will of God was a priority. In his early years, he thought he was doing the will of God by opposing Jesus and His followers. Paul, originally called Saul, had been an exceptional student trained by some of the top biblical scholars of his day. But after Saul's encounter with Jesus on the Damascus road, everything changed. Saul had encountered the risen Christ, and Jesus had asked Saul why was persecuting Him. Shaken to the core of his being, Saul was left blind. For three days, he wouldn't eat or drink anything. During this three-day period, the Holy Spirit showed him in a vision that a man named Ananias would come and place his hands on him to restore his sight. Then, Saul's vision became a living reality. Ananias came to Saul, restored his sight in Jesus' name, and told him in detail what had happened to him on the road to Damascus, even though Ananias wasn't even there. The only way that Ananias could have known what had happened was through the Holy Spirit.

I doubt that you could convince Paul that we should only use reason to apply scriptures to our lives. Paul would want us to know that the leadership of the Holy Spirit is absolutely essential in interpreting scriptures and in knowing the will of God. Saul, an avid student of the scriptures, thought he was obeying God by trying to destroy this Jesus movement when he was in fact moving in direct opposition to God's will. Jesus had warned his disciples that there would be those who would put them to death thinking that they were rendering a service to God (John 16:2). This is what Saul had done until his encounter with Jesus and until the Holy Spirit became real in his life.

Paul had a brilliant mind. When Paul gave his testimony to King Agrippa and to Festus about the resurrection of Jesus from the dead, Festus contended that Paul's great learning had driven him insane (Acts 26:19-27). In the book of Romans, Paul has this to say about the proper use of our minds:

> [5] For those who are *living* according to the flesh set their minds on the things of the flesh [which gratify the body], but those who are *living* according to the Spirit, [set their minds on] the things of the Spirit [His will and purpose]. [6] Now the mind of the flesh is death [both now and forever—because it pursues sin]; but the mind of the Spirit is life and peace [the spiritual well-being that comes from walking with God—both now and forever]. (Rom. 8:5-6 AMP)

Notice that Paul says that we are to set our minds on what the Spirit desires instead of saying that we should set the Spirit on what our minds desire. For Paul, the leadership of the Holy Spirit was not a vague concept that we talk about and only feel in a general kind of way. In fact, it was under the specific guidance of the Holy Spirit that Paul lived out his faith in Jesus. Can't you imagine that Paul was grateful that Ananias was willing to model what it looked like to obey the Holy Spirit's specific directions in coming to see him, even though Ananias' logical mind was likely screaming out, "No, don't go!" Through Ananias, Paul got to see someone who lived out what Paul was to teach later about subordinating one's reason to the leadership of the Holy Spirit. If even Paul, intellectually gifted as he was, needed the specific leadership of the Holy Spirit to come to know Jesus in a deeper way and then live for Him, wouldn't we today need more than just reason alone, and more than just scriptures alone, to help us effectively live out the will of God in our lives?

For us to become the men and women God has called us to be, we need to see that living in partnership with the Holy Spirit is essential to following Jesus. John was in the Spirit on the Lord's Day on the Island of Patmos when Jesus showed up in glory and power. John was awestruck by Jesus' appearance: so much so that it put him flat on the ground. To say that what followed was a time of revelation is an understatement. Toward the beginning of this revelation to John, Jesus gave some words of correction to speak to seven churches (Rev. 2, 3). By the way, they are words of correction for us as well. At the end of these messages to the each of the seven churches, this statement appears all seven times: "Anyone with ears to hear must listen to the Spirit and understand what he is saying to the churches" (NLT). Since it was this important to Jesus that we listen to the Holy Spirit, why not take the time to learn to listen to the Holy Spirit?

So, assuming we need the leadership of the Holy Spirit as much as Paul and John did, how do we position ourselves to receive the Holy Spirit's leadership?

First, let's look again at Acts 9 and the communication that Ananias received from the Holy Spirit:

> [10] In Damascus there was a disciple named Ananias. The Lord called to him in a vision, "Ananias!"

> "Yes, Lord," he answered.

> [11] The Lord told him, "Go to the house of Judas on Straight Street and ask for a man from Tarsus named Saul, for he is praying. 12 In a vision he has seen a man

named Ananias come and place his hands on him to restore his sight." (Acts 9:10-11)

Here, the Holy Spirit speaks to both Ananias and Saul in visions. In Saul's case the vision came while he was praying. In Ananias' case, whether or not he was praying when he received his vision is not specified. He could have been praying when he received this message from the Holy Spirit, but we don't know.

In the book of Acts, we are given a snapshot of the way that Peter followed the leadership of the Holy Spirit:

> [9] About noon the following day as they were on their journey and approaching the city, Peter went up on the roof to pray. [10] He became hungry and wanted something to eat, and while the meal was being prepared, he fell into a trance. [11] He saw heaven opened and something like a large sheet being let down to earth by its four corners. [12] It contained all kinds of four-footed animals, as well as reptiles and birds. [13] Then a voice told him, "Get up, Peter. Kill and eat."
>
> [14] "Surely not, Lord!" Peter replied. "I have never eaten anything impure or unclean."
>
> [15] The voice spoke to him a second time, "Do not call anything impure that God has made clean."
>
> [16] This happened three times, and immediately the sheet was taken back to heaven. (Acts 10:9-16)

Here, like Saul did, Peter received a vision from the Holy Spirit while he was praying. Prayer helps us so much in learning to receive direction from the Holy Spirit. Prayer helps us to get connected to the leadership of the Holy Spirit, because when we are praying, it becomes easier to set our minds and hearts on things above (Col. 3:1-2). Through prayer, we open the door to our hearts becoming connected to God's heart. Peter had heard the Great Commission of Jesus to go throughout the world and make disciples of all nations (Matt. 28:18-20). But it was the work of the Holy Spirit in this vision that helped Peter step into Jesus' worldwide mission. The Holy Spirit helped Peter apply what Jesus had commanded for his life. Now, through the leadership of the Holy Spirit, Jesus' commission had become a living reality for Peter.

While the Holy Spirit was speaking to Peter, God was at work in the life of a God-fearing Gentile by the name of Cornelius. Listen to how what Peter was receiving in prayer was to become a reality on earth as it is in heaven:

> [30] Cornelius answered: "Three days ago I was in my house praying at this hour, at three in the afternoon. Suddenly a man in shining clothes stood before me [31] and said, 'Cornelius, God has heard your prayer and remembered your gifts to the poor. [32] Send to Joppa for Simon who is called Peter. He is a guest in the home of Simon the tanner, who lives by the sea.' [33] So I sent for you immediately, and it was good of you to come. Now we are all here in the presence of God to listen to everything the Lord has commanded you to tell us." (Acts 10:30-33)

Interestingly, when we first read about the angel who appeared to Cornelius, the detail that this happened while he was praying was left out (Acts 10:1-8). But later when Cornelius tells Peter the story of what happened, we find out Cornelius was praying when the angel came to speak to him.

These scripture passages establish a few amazing precedents: the Holy Spirit communicates through visions, angels speak, and the Holy Spirit speaks in words. Were the words to Peter from an audible voice or were the words Peter heard on the inside? We aren't told one way or the other. Regardless of how the Holy Spirit spoke, prayer seems to be fundamental in setting the stage for the Holy Spirit to speak.

Here is another scripture from Acts in which the Holy Spirit speaks:

> [1] Now in the church at Antioch there were prophets and teachers: Barnabas, Simeon called Niger, Lucius of Cyrene, Manaen (who had been brought up with Herod the tetrarch) and Saul. [2] While they were worshiping the Lord and fasting, the Holy Spirit said, "Set apart for me Barnabas and Saul for the work to which I have called them." [3] So after they had fasted and prayed, they placed their hands on them and sent them off. (Acts 13:1-3)

In this passage, worship and fasting set the stage for the Holy Spirit to speak. To be sure, God in His mercy will often speak to people even when they are not seeking Him. But having said this, the Lord loves to respond to people when they are seeking Him with all their hearts, souls, minds, and strength. The disciples were seeking the Lord through worship and fasting, and the Holy Spirit spoke. After the disciples received direction from the Holy Spirit, prayer is highlighted as having been added to the mix of fasting and worship.

What we are given in these passages is just a glimpse of the Holy Spirit in action communicating the will of the Lord for the Lord's Kingdom business. It appears that the Holy Spirit's speaking is not limited to when people are praying, worshipping, or fasting, but it seems that these ways of seeking God are often rewarded with communication from above. It is interesting that Jesus' teaching on prayer in Luke 11 (the Lord's Prayer) is followed by teaching on the importance of asking, seeking, and knocking because our good Father loves to give the Holy Spirit to those that ask.

Regardless of denomination, who has not said that we should speak to God in prayer and that we should also learn to listen in prayer as well? All of this to say that listening to God in prayer is a powerful way to connect to what the Holy Spirit wants to say to us. We need the Holy Spirit to help us know what our specific Kingdom of God assignments are! We also desperately need revelation from the Holy Spirit so that we don't miss what God is saying to us from His Word (John 5:31-44).

Paul prayed in Ephesians 1 that believers would have a spirit of wisdom and revelation to know the Lord better. After first encountering listening prayer in my early forties, I found a short teaching on revelation knowledge, read it three times, and still had no clue what the person was talking about. At the time, I believed that the only way we could know things was through our five senses. What in the world is this spiritual form of knowing that they are talking about, I wondered? Also, what in the world is all this talk about the Holy Spirit speaking? I kept thinking that there had to be more to the Christian faith than I was experiencing, but it all felt so hard to understand. Many of the students that I went to seminary with made fun of "Holy Spirit types" so I found myself viewing people who talked about the ministry of the Holy Spirit with caution and suspicion. Yet, despite all my reservations and questions, I kept searching. As a college student, I had attended a time of worship at a house church meeting. The atmosphere was electric with the power of the Holy Spirit as the participants worshipped. The echo of this was still in my heart years later and the longing for more than what I was presently experiencing would just not go away.

The supernatural way that the gospel moved forward in the book of Acts is incredible. The question that contemporary people have to struggle with is this: is what happened in the early church only for the early church or is it for us as well? Early in ministry, I used to preach a sermon on the book of Acts called "The Holy Spirit Adventure." I would always think of that worship service I had attended in college when I preached this message. I will never forget the description I heard about a certain pastor. Someone said that this pastor was like a travel agent telling people about beautiful lands that he had never visited personally. As I look back now, I honestly must say that I, too, was a travel agent telling people about beautiful lands that I had never visited personally as I preached this message on the book of Acts. The message did however express a longing in my heart that would just not go away.

It is one thing to hear stories about how God has spoken to others but it is something entirely different when God uses one of His servants to speak the words of the Holy Spirit to us. One day I was invited to the small chapel at our campus ministry where I was the campus minister to attend a meeting given by a man that had learned to hear from the Lord. So, with a bit of nervousness and excitement, I attended. After the meeting was over, somehow I had been ushered in front of this guy to receive whatever the Holy Spirit might want to say to me. As the man started speaking, I began to weep. He was saying things that had been buried in my heart. The Holy Spirit was making His presence known to me at a deep heart level. Even now, after all of these years, I still remember some of what was said.

He said that I had laid ambition down and that I was going after God. I had done that; I had really done that. He said that I had been to this crossroads many times before but that now I was here to stay. As I have said, this journey started when I was exposed to the Holy Spirit's presence in worship as a college student, but at that point I did not pursue the ministry of the Holy Spirit in my life. Later in my twenties, I had started moving in the ministry of the Holy Spirit when a friend of mine was healed of brain cancer. But later, Lee, a member of the church where I was the pastor, whom we all loved, died in spite of all of our prayers for healing. I concluded that while the ministry of the Holy Spirit was real, it was not for me because I was just too ordinary. But now, for a third season in my life, I was engaging in the ministry of the Holy Spirit, and this time I had decided that I was going to go all in regardless of what happened. The last thing I remembered him praying for me was that I would mentor many young people. At that time, I had not mentored anyone. But as of this writing, I have had the privilege of mentoring so many young people.

Wow, was the Word from the Holy Spirit ever true! I am still amazed.

So, finally, after fifteen years of thinking that the New Testament ministry of the Holy Spirit was just not for me because of how incredibly ordinary I was, I had begun to learn to listen to the Lord in prayer. One day I asked the Lord if there was a bible verse that I could give to my friend Dave, an awesome campus minister who was part of our campus minister's prayer fellowship. Psalm 32:8 flashed in my mind and the words the Holy Spirit put in my heart were accompanied with great peace. Later that day, I told Dave that I had listened in prayer and received Psalm 32:8 to give to him. Tears started streaming down Dave's face. He got out his scripture card packet and showed me the verse that had been in the window of the packet for a couple of weeks. Yes, it was Psalm 32:8! Listen to how the Lord was speaking to us both from His Word and from the leading of the Holy Spirit: "I will instruct you and teach you the way you should go; I will counsel you and watch over you" (Psalm 32:8).

God was demonstrating to us how awesome it is when His Word is applied by the leading of the Holy Spirit. To be the men and women of God that we are called to be, we need both the Holy Bible and the Holy Spirit to equip us to do all that God has called us to do. Listening prayer is an active dialogue with the Lord where we pour out our hearts to the Lord and then He speaks to us through the Holy Spirit.

Multiple voices, one prayer

Michael, a college student at a major university, had been prayed for a number of times with listening prayer. Michael wanted to move into listening prayer but thought that this would be impossible for somebody like him. But then the impossible happened and he moved into listening prayer. Michael was leading a Bible study with six guys in Lexington, Kentucky. Michael called me on the phone and then he called Tommy, a college student at another university that had moved into listening prayer, on another phone. I was in Louisville at the time and Tommy was in Bowling Green. Michael prayed for all six guys in person and then Tommy and I prayed for each of them over the two phones that were being passed around. I prayed a different prayer for each guy, but found out later that the prayers I prayed were the same ones Michael had prayed for each guy which also were the same ones Tommy had prayed for each guy. None of us heard what the others were praying. Yet we each listened to the Holy Spirit and then prayed essentially the same prayers each individual guy apparently needed to hear. I share this to say that listening prayer through Jesus' mighty name is real!

I was on a youth retreat with Pastor Paul and a group of his high school guys came into the designated prayer area for me to pray for them. I struggled through the whole prayer time. My mind was raising one doubt after another as I prayed for the guys. The Holy Spirit was putting words in my heart yet my mind was arguing with everything. These are the kind of thoughts that were hammering me as I was listening on the inside: you are really tired; you are probably off track with the Holy Spirit; what you are praying is just a bunch of general stuff that you have prayed over and over again for other people. After the prayer time, I felt like a beginner in listening prayer yet again. Then, Pastor Paul came over to me and told me, "Those guys you just prayed for are really freaked out. They had just shared with one another what they needed the Lord to help them with and they just heard pretty much word for word from you what they had just said." The Holy Spirit was teaching me yet again to stay in childlike trust when I am listening in prayer and not to yield to my skeptical mind.

Perhaps your mind is filled with many questions about all of this just as mine was when I first found out that listening to the Lord in prayer was even possible. Perhaps you have had negative experiences with "Holy Spirit types" whose pride and condescending attitude turned you off which made the possibility of the Holy Spirit speaking seem even more difficult to believe. I had those experiences, too. But why let someone else's immaturity prevent you from receiving a great blessing from God? Just for the record, the Apostle Paul had quite a bit to say to some immature folks whose character had not yet caught up with what God was doing through their lives. You can read about it in 1 Corinthians. One of my favorite things to say on Pentecost Sunday is that the work of the Holy Spirit is not a spiritual merit badge of spiritual superiority. Instead, Pentecost is evidence that God's servants can't possibly get the job done unless the Lord steps in and helps them through the power of the Holy Spirit.

In Acts 17:10-13 we hear the story about the noble Bereans who went home to study the Word of God to see if what Paul was saying was true. As a result of their openness of heart, the Lord gave them the assurance that the gospel of Jesus was from the Lord. I would encourage you to continue to study the Word with openness of heart the way that the Bereans did. If you have grown up in a tradition where the Holy Spirit was talked about as a concept to be understood rather than a partnership to be lived out, there is more. Or, if you have been a part of a religious tradition where you have been taught that the Holy Spirit stopped speaking with the apostles, there is more. Know that tremendous joy awaits you as you learn to obey Jesus from both His commands (John 15:9-11) and from the leading of the Holy Spirit (Acts 5:32) working together in your life.

Seen and known by Jesus

Kelsey was attending a workshop on listening prayer that I was leading. She had seen some of the fruit of this type of ministry but she wanted to make sure that what was being done was Word-based. She was also seeking confirmation in her heart through prayer that this was from the Lord. Kelsey took lots of notes that day, but she had decided that she did not want to receive prayer because she wanted to go home and think about it. Just as worship was concluding and the time was coming to a close, Kelsey was handed a phone so that Julie could pray for her. She nervously agreed to have Julie to pray for her. What stood out the most about the prayer time with Julie was the great love that the Father had for her. This love opened up Kelsey's heart to experience more listening prayer as well that day. Kelsey said that she felt seen and known by Jesus and she was overwhelmed with how loved she was by Him. She said that she experienced the most beautiful heart connection with the Father that she had ever experienced in her Christian walk.

Sometime later after this initial introduction to listening prayer, Kelsey initiated a Harvest event for young adults where she opened the way for listening prayer ministry to be offered. She got to see lines of young adults experiencing being seen, known, and loved by the Father through listening prayer. Now Kelsey prays for people with listening prayer and gets to be one of those helping others discover how loved they are by Jesus. She also gets to partner with the Holy Spirit so that young adults will experience the call of God on their lives and will follow Jesus into the amazing adventures that the Lord has lined up for them.

As a kid, I liked the churches I grew up in. However, I wasn't particularly fond of the day that I fell asleep in Sunday school with my eyes wide open (a skill that I developed early at church—trust me, as a pastor, I see you out there…), because while I was sleeping a couple of guys tied my belt to the chair. It was not a pretty sight when I tried to get up to leave. Even now I have the amazing ability to fall asleep during a prayer meeting and wake up praying—much to the delight of the young adults who are present. To this very day, I seem to be a photographic opportunity on trips when I fall asleep: go figure! It's the story that never ends; trust me!

I digress, but this being said, there were two events at church that I particularly liked. The first event was covered-dish dinners. I used to stand by the table in advance of the blessing so I could study the various foods being offered and devise my plan. The second notable event was the occasional special Sunday evening worship services when we sang old hymns. It was indeed a joyful noise and we all seemed to enjoy it, except for the musicians with perfect pitch. Their pain was real. At the time, I didn't realize that one of my favorite hymns called "In the Garden" would speak about the relationship with Jesus that I and so many of us would get to experience through listening prayer:

In the Garden, by C. Austin Miles

Verse 1
I come to the garden alone,
While the dew is still on the roses;
And the voice I hear, falling on my ear,
The Son of God discloses.

Verse 2
He speaks, and the sound of His voice,
Is so sweet the birds hush their singing,
And the melody that He gave to me
Within my heart is ringing.

Verse 3
I'd stay in the garden with Him
Though the night around me be falling,
But He bids me go; through the voice of woe,
His voice to me is calling.

Chorus
And He walks with me,
And He talks with me,
And He tells me I am His own;
And the joy we share as we tarry there,
None other has ever known.

Jeannie is someone that gets to experience what this song is talking about. She loves to listen to Jesus' voice in prayer and it is a good day when she gets to pray for you!

I first interacted with Jeannie when she was a faculty recruiter at a Christian university. She sent me the nicest rejection letter to my request to teach as an adjunct instructor. (There for you, Jeannie...) We got connected later when Jeannie listened to the Lord in prayer and contacted me about an open chaplaincy position. The crazy thing is that Pastor David had received in prayer for me to have an open heart about a job opportunity that would be offered in the next week. He told me, "Please disregard this if for some reason I missed it." Four days later Jeannie contacted me about the chaplaincy position. Listening prayer just never gets old—trust me!

Here is one of Jeannie's favorite listening prayer stories:

Plans to quit, changed

"The Lord led me to a student during an evening chapel service at a Christian university. She did not appear to be very engaged nor paying attention to what was going on during the service. I sensed that I was to pray for her. I knew that whatever that the Holy Spirit had me pray was hitting her hard—she was just overwhelmed and was crying.

"It wasn't until a week or two later that I found out what the Lord did to her. She was on the verge of leaving the university and had plans to quit at the end of that week. She felt hopeless and was very discouraged. But when the Lord

ministered to her that evening, it was as if I had prayed about all her struggles and she really experienced His deep love for her. It changed her heart and mind and she decided to stay. A few weeks later, she accepted Christ."

The Holy Spirit is often called the Holy Spirit of Truth. I have seen skeptics, agnostics, and atheists become intrigued and curious after being prayed for through listening prayer because the Holy Spirit of Truth spoke to them at a deep heart level. Our Campus Thirst prayer team asks to pray for people in public quite a bit and sometimes people will say something like, "Yeah, go ahead if it means something to you." It is an interesting phenomenon to watch someone who has come to believe that Christianity is a delusional fairy tale suddenly experience the love and peace of Jesus in their hearts. Sometimes people will respond, "Funny that you mention that, what you said is actually quite true."

I was visiting Pastor Daniel and we were getting ready for an evening of worship and prayer on a university campus. I was telling Judy about the joy of praying for students on the sidewalk. She had been an ambassador for the school and was very good at meeting people. I told her that she would enjoy seeing the Lord touch students through listening prayer. Suddenly, I said, "Hey, we have about a half an hour before we start here, let's take a few minutes and let me show you what this looks like." In Judy's own words, this is a little bit of what she got to see:

Sheer truth proclaimed

"We were walking around campus. The first student that we prayed for was a younger well-put together guy. We stopped him to ask to pray for him, and he agreed. After Pastor Tim prayed for him, the guy shook his hand and thanked him. And I like this story because there weren't

necessarily tears shed, or a huge visible miracle that happened, but you could still tell that his heart was being touched by God's words for him. The way he thanked Pastor Tim with a firm handshake and direct eye contact spoke to the encounter with the supernatural loving God that he just had. The other memory that stands out in this time of praying for people was of the interaction with two foreign exchange students. They were walking by, and we asked if we could pray for them. They didn't know what prayer was, and after explaining it to them, one of the students agreed, while the other was somewhat dismissive and kind of laughed it off. However, as Pastor Tim started praying for the first friend, the other friend was listening in, and you could tell he was shocked as words of sheer truth were being proclaimed over his friend from a complete stranger. After the first prayer, we asked if we could pray for the second friend, and he was much more receptive. We prayed for him too, and they both left feeling blessed and intrigued about what just happened. It was a great way to open a door for them to our Lord!"

When I first began to experience listening prayer, the biggest takeaway for me was that Jesus sees us, that He loves us, and that He desperately wants a relationship with us. For those of you who are reluctant to move into experiencing listening prayer, I would say that the love of Jesus is what will surprise you the most. When you receive in prayer the Lord telling you how much He loves you, it will change everything. At this point, I have seen Jesus love on thousands of people through listening prayer. I wouldn't trade this for anything.

In some parts of the world, it is not uncommon for groups of Christians to be put to death if they are discovered gathering to worship Jesus. For these Christians, hearing Jesus' voice in prayer is essential for survival. If they announce a meeting, the information can get into the wrong hands and death will be certain. So, what they do is to listen in prayer and then the Holy Spirit will tell them what day the meeting will be, where it will be, and what time the meeting will take place. Then, like clockwork, the Holy Spirit will gather the faithful to worship Jesus as King, Lord, and Savior. I guess you could call these folks extreme sheep for following Jesus the way that they do. What if hearing Jesus' voice through the leading of the Holy Spirit the way that these folks do became a reality in our lives? What if the testimony of these extreme sheep is to teach us a new normal? What if learning to hear Jesus' voice through the Holy Spirit speaking to us in prayer is really that important?

I have often told people that if someone offered me a billion dollars with the only stipulation being that I could no longer hear the voice of the Holy Spirit in prayer, I would laugh at the offer and walk away. There just isn't enough money that would make it worth giving up this Kingdom of God treasure. So, what do you think: are you ready to go looking for treasure?

Dear Lord, I ask that You would do whatever You want to do in my life even if this means making me different from what I grew up with. I ask You, Lord, to give me an openness of heart to listening prayer if this is something that You want to be a part of my life. It is my heartfelt desire, Lord, that You would make a miracle out of my life. In Jesus' name, I pray. Amen.

CHAPTER 2

Why Listen in Prayer?

Jesus longs to have a relationship with us—a close, personal relationship. Listen to the incredible encounter that John had with Jesus on the Island of Patmos when John was in the Spirit on the Lord's day:

> [12] I turned around to see the voice that was speaking to me. And when I turned I saw seven golden lampstands, [13] and among the lampstands was someone like a son of man, dressed in a robe reaching down to his feet and with a golden sash around his chest. [14] The hair on his head was white like wool, as white as snow, and his eyes were like blazing fire. [15] His feet were like bronze glowing in a furnace, and his voice was like the sound of rushing waters. [16] In his right hand he held seven stars, and coming out of his mouth was a sharp, double-edged sword. His face was like the sun shining in all its brilliance.
>
> [17] When I saw him, I fell at his feet as though dead. Then he placed his right hand on me and said: "Do not be afraid. I am the First and the Last. [18] I am the Living One; I was dead, and now look, I am alive

forever and ever! And I hold the keys of death and Hades." (Rev. 1:12-17)

Listen: Experience Intimacy with Jesus

Jesus followed up this encounter with John with the incredible revelation that we know now as the book of Revelation in the New Testament. Listen to Jesus' heart cry for a personal relationship with His people in his message to the church of Laodicea:

> [20] Here I am! I stand at the door and knock. If anyone hears my voice and opens the door, I will come in and eat with that person, and they with me.
>
> [21] To the one who is victorious, I will give the right to sit with me on my throne, just as I was victorious and sat down with my Father on his throne. [22] Whoever has ears, let them hear what the Spirit says to the churches. (Rev. 3:20-22)

Why learn to listen in prayer? Jesus wants us to experience closeness with Him that goes beyond what we can imagine. We have no idea how much Jesus loves us. We really don't. As you move into listening prayer, Jesus will make His love known to you in ways that you would have never dreamed possible. You will hear me say this over and over again: what will surprise you the most about listening prayer is how much Jesus loves you! His love changes us from the inside out.

One night I heard someone call my name loudly while I was sleeping. I woke up instantly and then the Lord spoke into my heart, "I just woke you up to tell you that I love you." As a kid, I loved the Samuel story from the Old Testament in which the Lord spoke to Samuel at night. Now, the Lord was doing something for me that He knew would mean so much to me. The Lord longs to have intimacy and fellowship with us and to share His voice with us. But we need to understand how much we desperately need Him. The church in Laodicea had become self-reliant instead of God reliant. They had begun to trust their own resources instead of trusting in the Lord. Jesus gave the church in Laodicea the invitation to repent and then to know Him through listening to His voice. So, the first incredible blessing of listening prayer is intimacy and fellowship with Jesus, the lover of our soul. The next blessing is to see others come to know Jesus as Savior, Lord, and best friend through listening prayer.

Listen: Help Others Know Jesus as Lord

It was revealed to Saul that Jesus was the Son of God on the road to Damascus. During the three-day period after meeting the risen Christ, the Holy Spirit, speaking to him in prayer, confirmed again to Saul that Jesus was the Son of God (Acts 9:10-19). The purpose of listening prayer is not to bring attention to the person praying, but to focus the attention of the person who is being prayed for on Jesus as the Son of God. As part of our ministry that goes on to university campuses to pray for students, I find that students are typically surprised when we ask them if we can pray for them and they are even more surprised when the prayers are personal to their lives. Our desire and hope in praying for students is that a seed gets planted about how real God is and that they will come to know Jesus as the Son of God:

> [5] What, after all, is Apollos? And what is Paul? Only servants, through whom you came to believe—as the Lord has assigned to each his task. [6] I planted the seed, Apollos watered it, but God has been making it grow. [7] So neither the one who plants nor the one who waters is anything, but only God, who makes things grow. (1 Cor. 3:5-7)

I will never forget the time a student called me a few days after he was prayed for on campus. He told me that after he had been prayed for, he went to church and was born again! Listening prayer can be used mightily in helping us be faithful to the Great Commission mandate from Jesus:

> [18] Then Jesus came to them and said, "All authority in heaven and on earth has been given to me. [19] Therefore go and make disciples of all nations, baptizing them in the name of the Father and of the Son and of the Holy Spirit, [20] and teaching them to obey everything I have commanded you. And surely I am with you always, to the very end of the age." (Matt. 28:18-20)

Go fishing!

Rob believes that Jesus can do anything. What Jesus did for Rob is absolutely miraculous and is why he has the faith to believe that Jesus can do anything. Rob loves to pray for people, share his testimony, and the gospel whenever he gets the opportunity. Recently, he was fishing and received in prayer to go down river before he left. He followed this direction. He went down river, and out of the woods came four guys in camo who needed some help. When they left Rob, Rob said that you could see the whites of their eyes. What had happened to cause their surprised reactions? Rob had prayed for all four of them with listening prayer and he had shared his testimony. While they weren't ready yet to accept the gospel for their lives, the prayers that Rob had prayed for them, his testimony, and the gospel had shaken them to their cores.

☙

The small detail of the look in some one's eyes is sometimes all the evidence we need that God is working through listening prayer. The curiosity and surprise on people's faces after they receive listening prayer will inspire you to keep sowing seeds of the gospel into people's lives.

God is real

A group of college students and young adults from Ohio were attending a high school youth retreat to help provide leadership and they managed to convince Lily to come along with them. Lily had grown up in the church, but because of some disappointments she had experienced in her life she had a hard time believing that God was real. On the trip, she was regretting spending a week of vacation time to go on the retreat, but she couldn't escape because she had been talked out of bringing her own car and had travelled with the group in a van. During worship, some of the kids were receiving prayer. Lily decided to try talking to the Lord; she said that if the Lord could show her that He was real that she would surrender her life to Him. Suddenly, someone in the row behind her asked if he could pray for Lily. She couldn't even see the person but said yes. The person started the prayer with the statement "God is real," repeating it ten times and getting a little louder as he went. Lily was crying hard before the prayer was over. She ended up giving her life to Christ. Listening prayer had shown her that Jesus really was the Son of God!

Many people have a profound respect for Jesus and see him as a great teacher or even as a prophet of God, but don't believe in Him as God's One and Only Son. But C.S. Lewis was right: Jesus must be Lord, a liar, or a lunatic. How could Jesus be a true prophet if what He said here was not true?

> [5] Thomas said to him, "Lord, we don't know where you are going, so how can we know the way?"

> [6] Jesus answered, "I am the way and the truth and the

life. No one comes to the Father except through me. [7] If you really know me, you will know my Father as well. From now on, you do know him and have seen him."

[8] Philip said, "Lord, show us the Father and that will be enough for us."

[9] Jesus answered: "Don't you know me, Philip, even after I have been among you such a long time? Anyone who has seen me has seen the Father. How can you say, 'Show us the Father'? [10] Don't you believe that I am in the Father, and that the Father is in me? The words I say to you I do not speak on my own authority. Rather, it is the Father, living in me, who is doing his work. [11] Believe me when I say that I am in the Father and the Father is in me; or at least believe on the evidence of the works themselves." (John 14:9-11)

C.S. Lewis' point is that we can't have it both ways. Either Jesus is the Son of God, or a crazy person, or the worst kind of liar. This nice, polite categorization of Jesus as a simply admirable person and great teacher is not logically possible if He was, as he claimed, the Son of God. So here is the issue: if Jesus really is the Son of God, how I choose to live my life in relationship to Jesus and what I choose to believe about Jesus suddenly becomes all-important. If Jesus is only a prophet or merely a good teacher, I can show Jesus some respect but I can take or leave what He has to say. In other words, if Jesus isn't the Son of God then what He said really has no bearing on the decisions I make or how I live my life. If Jesus is only a teacher or a prophet who is one among many, Jesus has no ultimate claim on my life. But if Jesus is the Son of God, what I decide about whether I ask Jesus to forgive me of my sins and to be the leader of my life has eternal consequences.

In the Garden of Eden, Satan managed to get Adam and

Eve to believe his lies. Human beings have continued to be fooled by Satan's lies ever since. But God in His mercy knows how susceptible our intellects are to skepticism, cynicism, and unbelief toward God's truths. So Jesus told us that the day was coming when the Holy Spirit would be at work to convince us of the truth about Jesus as the Christ:

> [7] But very truly I tell you, it is for your good that I am going away. Unless I go away, the Advocate will not come to you; but if I go, I will send him to you. [8] When he comes, he will prove the world to be in the wrong about sin and righteousness and judgment: [9] about sin, because people do not believe in me; [10] about righteousness, because I am going to the Father, where you can see me no longer; [11] and about judgment, because the prince of this world now stands condemned.
>
> [12] I have much more to say to you, more than you can now bear. [13] But when he, the Spirit of truth, comes, he will guide you into all the truth. (John 16:12-13)

When we listen to the Lord in prayer on behalf of other people, we join the Holy Spirit's ministry to convince them that Jesus really is the Son of God.

You are not invisible to Jesus

Jenna shared that she had asked the Lord for something to give to a lady who was in her 80's. In prayer, Jenna heard a street name, and she asked the lady if this particular street name meant something to her. This lady told her that she and her husband owned a piece of property on that road. This lady went from being an agnostic to believing in Jesus as the Christ because of this simple word from the Lord.

Jenna talked to another woman who said that she was ready to commit suicide because of the incredible trauma she had been through from the ages of 10 to 17. She said that her religion was whatever "sounded good." Jenna told her, "Let's see if Jesus will tell me something about you that sounds good." Jenna told the woman that she saw a picture of her sitting in a field of flowers for comfort and to tell her that Jesus was there with her. Sitting in a field of flowers was the one place that this lady had felt comfort in the midst of the trauma that she went through. She accepted Christ after that!

Jenna also prayed listening prayer on behalf of two other guys. One of the guys received four specific pieces of information about his life but still said, "There is no God." Another man who received the Holy Spirit's ministry on his behalf started weeping, but said he wasn't in a position to accept Christ at the moment because he was so broken. But, maybe these men who said no to the Lord at that moment in time will yet come home to Jesus as their Savior and Lord. Regardless of whether these men choose to say yes to the Lord, you can rest assured that the Holy Spirit will continue to be at work on their hearts. The Lord is continually at work giving opportunities for people to believe in God's beloved Son Jesus through the ministry of the Holy Spirit.

Jesus knows our personal situations

One evening a group of college students got together in a dorm room. Some of them were getting ready to go on a mission trip. So, John decided to step out in faith and asked if he could pray for everyone with listening prayer. During the prayer for the last student that John prayed for, he felt like he needed to take a bold step because of what the Holy Spirit was putting on his heart to pray for her. He prayed that the Lord would help her with a difficult family situation.

He said that the Lord could see how her parent's divorce was hurting her and that her broken relationship with her dad was making it difficult for her to believe in God and in Jesus. She wept as John prayed because he knew nothing about her personal situation. Afterwards she asked John how he knew. He told her the Holy Spirit was letting her know how real Jesus is. A couple of weeks later this student accepted Jesus as her Savior. Don't you want to help people know Jesus as their Lord and Savior through listening prayer?

Listen: Hear His Call

My mentor, Dr. Harold Kastner, used to call God's plans our daily assignments. Luke 9:23 talks about surrendering our will to Jesus' will on a daily basis. Listening prayer helps us to move into God's daily assignments for our lives. In Acts 13:1-3 we read about the Holy Spirit speaking about one of the Holy Spirit assignments that was part of the calling that the Lord had for Paul and Barnabas' lives. Just as the Holy Spirit revealed God's purposes and plans for the early disciples' lives, the Holy Spirit wants to reveal God's calling on our lives as well. How exciting that we can discover the call of God on our lives as we learn to listen in prayer!

Julie learned the call of God on her life through listening prayer. Listen to her story:

Victory over fear

Julie was a music major at Belmont University. She is an amazingly gifted worship leader. But the Lord surprised Julie: she was led by the Holy Spirit to change her major from music to nursing. She was given a dream about working at a hospital in Lexington, Kentucky. Here was the problem: in her pharmacology class, she got a D- on the first test. On the second test she got a low F. Her test anxiety was so bad that she would get sick during the tests. Even after a great deal of study, she would freeze during the test because of her intense fear. In order to stay in the nursing program, her instructor told her that she would have to make A's on the rest of her exams. That day she felt totally defeated and her plan for the evening was to stay at home and eat cookie dough. She decided maybe she wasn't supposed to be a nurse after all.

Against her will, her friend convinced her to go to church that evening. In the middle of the message, the guest pastor stopped and said, "The Lord is telling me that there is a person here who wants to be a nurse and they don't think that they can do it. If that's you, would you please raise your hand." Another girl raised her hand immediately, so Julie kind of halfway raised her hand. The pastor called both of them to the front. The pastor prayed for the other girl first and when he got to Julie he said, "Oh, it's you. Would you like this fear to leave?" Julie nodded her head through her tears and during the prayer Julie felt something leave her. She made A's on the rest of her exams. Her teacher pulled her aside and told her that she hated to ask her this, but wanted to know if she had been cheating. After Julie told her the story, her instructor said, "I want that guy to pray for me too!"

ﷺ

As it worked out, Julie ended up working at the hospital that she dreamed about. Imagine Julie's excitement when she saw the inside of the hospital for the first time and it looked like what she had already seen in the dream. Yet, for the first couple of months, the work situation was so difficult that she was begging the Lord to let her quit. Finally, one of the more established nurses befriended her. As it turned out, this new friend became a Christian largely through Julie's influence. One day Julie was in the break room on a Sunday, and I ended up getting to pray for a number of the nurses over the phone with listening prayer. They had to send out for a box of tissues because the love of Jesus was touching their hearts. Here is the miracle that happened. Julie started a bible study at her house for the nurses every other week for over a year. It was my privilege to lead the bible study and after every session Julie and I would pray for all of the nurses along with Tommy when he was able to join us. A number of these nurses gave their lives to Jesus. The Holy Spirit helped Julie get past her fear and the Lord used her to accomplish His purposes in a strategic mission field. The Holy Spirit wants to help move us into the center of God's calling for our lives!

Paul was one of the nurses that attended this Bible study prayer time. This was a very difficult season of Paul's life. He said that he deeply appreciated the listening prayer time with Julie, Tommy, and I at these sessions and that it had built his faith and hope. Now turn the clock ahead a couple of years when Paul attended a listening prayer conference that we were doing in the Seattle area. Listen to what happened as Paul began to step out in faith to do listening prayer:

God can use you!

"At the conclusion of the event, Pastor Tim and others divided into two prayer groups and there was a long line for each to receive prayer. Desiring to listen and pray, but still doubting my ability to hear with clarity, I hid myself in the back corner. Although, at the same time, I was hopeful someone would ask me to pray. A young lady walked in my direction and asked me to pray for her and her back. I asked her name and immediately prayed as Pastor Tim had instructed. I enjoyed hearing and sharing the love the Father had for her. As I was praying I saw a picture of a heavy weight. It was a block-style weight with a big steel handle on top of it. A chain was attached to the handle and the chain

was attached to her lower back. Only Jesus could sever that chain and He was there and I could see the chain being shattered with one swipe of His sword. Not wanting the weight to reattach itself to her, I listened for the Holy Spirit's direction as to what to do with the weight. He wanted it sent to the foot of the cross and buried beneath it. I enjoyed seeing it buried, unable to bother her again.

"A while later, she came to me again and showed me her back brace. Little did I know she was wearing one prior to our prayer and then she stated that she was healed."

Here is the reality; you never completely lose the feeling of being a beginner at listening prayer. This is a good thing because the feeling can keep us humble if we will let it. The important thing is to take the risk of faith and to begin.

Melissa was in a listening prayer Bible study group for college students. Listen to Melissa's story:

Ice skating vision

"When I was first learning listening prayer, I was practicing on my friend Hannah, and I got a picture for her. I saw her ice skating at a rink and she was really wobbly and all over the place at first, but as she kept going she started getting stronger and better, able to not wobble around so much. But when I saw this I thought to myself, 'Well that's weird. That can't be from God. How can ice skating have any spiritual meaning?' I tried to ignore it and hear something else, but it wouldn't go away, so finally I told her. She just stared at me for a few seconds and then said, 'You're the fourth person to pray that for me.' So even though my mind was saying it couldn't possibly be God, it most definitely was."

When people first start moving into listening prayer they feel like ice skaters learning to skate. Kelli's desire is to be in the middle of the Lord's will for her life. As she prayed about whether to take a new job, she got a picture in prayer of an open door along with the peace of the Lord. She also got confirmation from another prayer warrior so she moved out in faith and made the tough move. Grace prayed for a girl for the first time and saw the word *mom* as she prayed and then received that the past won't happen again. The girl began to weep and then shared what had been going on in her family. Ruth was prayed for with listening prayer and she received that part of her calling was to minister to people who were older than her and that folks who were older would be drawn to her. Later on that year, she ended up leading a Bible study for women who were ten to fifteen years older than she! She also got to pray for an older co-worker who wept when she recognized the love of Jesus for her during a very difficult transition in her life. You know you want to do this! The important thing is to just begin, even though you may doubt that God could actually use someone like you. But first, as you continue to read, let the Lord put a fire in your heart as we continue to talk at this point about some of the purposes of listening prayer.

Jim is an awesome prayer warrior who often prays for me right before I get ready to preach the gospel and tell people about how awesome Jesus is. Listen to this experience that he and his wife Rachel had as they were continuing to seek the Lord's will for their lives:

The wrong keyboard

"In May of 2012 my wife Rachel, while sitting and typing at her computer, heard that she was 'sitting at the wrong keyboard.' She was working at the time as an administrator for an online college. Just a few days later, I was driving across the state for a meeting of conference athletic directors. I had probably spent close to an hour praying in

the spirit when I clearly heard the voice of Yahweh tell me, 'Rachel is going to lose her job. It will look like this is something from the enemy, but it is not. I am repositioning her so that you can do what you need to do right now. Do not be afraid for this is of me.' Sure enough, a couple of weeks later Rachel received a call letting her know that she would not be able to keep her position due to restructuring. What we didn't know then was that Rachel losing her job ultimately allowed her to finish writing twelve songs that Yahweh had placed on her heart a year earlier. That probably would not have happened if she was still working. While at the time this was a distressing event, since Rachel's job loss meant losing half our income, it was incredibly reassuring to find out about it in advance and to know it was from God and not the enemy."

ﻋﻠﻰ

I have a story about another amazing Melissa. Melissa had a tremendous call of God on her life. She was married to a pastor and was the mother of two small boys. But Melissa had a problem: she had a very aggressive form of cancer. I tell her story next:

Called to witness

The week before she was to begin her bone marrow transplant we met at a local bookstore to visit. Melissa shared how she loved to witness about Jesus to other cancer patients in the hospital waiting room. She said that it is kind of hard to tell a young bald lady to shut up, so she took the opportunity to share whenever possible. One day a lady told Melissa as she was witnessing, "Sit right here, I'm going to go get my husband. He needs to talk to you!" She told me that she had always pictured herself as being in the palm of the Lord's hand. One of the listening prayers that had been prayed for her was that she was right in the palm of the Lord's hand. Through this listening prayer, the Lord had confirmed that a huge part of her calling was to teach people how to be close to Jesus. The visit in the bookstore that day was incredible but there is one moment that I will never forget. At one point, Melissa leaned forward and spoke with great intensity and passion. She said, "I want to live with all my heart, to continue to serve the Lord, and to raise my kids. But if my death will bring more people to Jesus than my life, then bring it!!!"

Melissa loved listening prayer and would receive prayer even when she was really unable to see anyone. Staff from all over the hospital would come to see her because she was truly an unforgettable person. I will never forget standing in a line with hundreds of people at the funeral home waiting to pay respects to Melissa's family with her words ringing in my ears. That day we met in the bookstore Melissa told me that if she didn't make it that she wanted me to tell her story. I have taken this commission very seriously so that is why I am sharing her testimony here. Melissa was all about helping people get close to Jesus. This was the Lord's call was on her life. Paul's words remind me so much of Melissa:

> [20] I eagerly expect and hope that I will in no way be ashamed, but will have sufficient courage so that now as always Christ will be exalted in my body, whether by life or by death. [21] For to me, to live is Christ and to die is gain. (Phil. 1:20-21)

Listen: Praying for Others

A motivating reason to move into listening prayer is that it helps us to pray in unison with Jesus' prayers for people as He intercedes for them: "Who is he that condemns? Christ Jesus, who died—more than that, who was raised to life—is at the right hand of God and is also interceding for us" (Rom. 8:34 NIV).

My mentor, Brother Harold, was thankful for the prayers of a woman who interceded. Listen to this:

Bows and arrows

Brother Harold was led by the Holy Spirit to travel to over 65 nations. Once, when he was traveling through Africa, his interpreter became alarmed when Brother Harold was laying hands on people as he prayed for healing. A commotion rose among the men in the community. Many people were receiving supernatural healings, but there was a problem. The interpreter had neglected to tell Brother Harold an important detail: it was an offense for a man other than a husband, priest, or king to touch a woman. The punishment? Being shot by bow and arrow. Despite the rising unrest among the men, Brother Harold heard in prayer to continue praying and laying hands on people, so he moved forward, unfazed. The men eventually asked Brother Harold to come outside and they offered him the gift of a Guinea hen. At first Brother Harold didn't want to take the hen. But his interpreter told him that he really should take the hen. The men brought him the gift because they had decided that Brother Harold must be a priest, and in their culture, only a priest or a king could eat a Guinea hen. Given his priestly status, they didn't have to kill him. Later when Brother Harold returned home, he learned that one of his intercessors had seen a vision of bows and arrows pointed at him and had prayed for his safety. This prayer for safety had been prayed at exactly the same time when this incident was taking place.

As a college student, I encountered skeptics who caused me to doubt whether I should continue to believe in Jesus. I had respect for Jesus, but I had begun to live for myself rather than for the Lord. I was empty and miserable but continued in my rebellion anyway. When I was home on break one summer, my Grandma Pink (her red hair looked pink to us kids) was visiting and she asked me what I thought about Jesus. My answer was less than substantial. My mom encouraged me to visit our next-door neighbor, Mrs. Lambert. I didn't want to, but I acquiesced. She was close to 90, but her face was absolutely radiant with light. At one point in the conversation, she said this to me: "Honey, I just talked to Jesus this morning!" Thinking back now, I realize I was the target of some serious intercession at that point in my life. Well, it worked: in a short time, I became profoundly disillusioned with the way I was living my life and decided to follow Jesus.

When I hit my forties, I was a pastor for college students but was once again experiencing emptiness. Something was wrong; I was going through the motions and didn't know how to fix the problem. Once again, as He had when I was a college student, the Lord raised up intercessors that prayed for me. Some loving students of mine would tell me quite often that they had been praying for me. I think they must have taken turns sitting in my chair and asking for the fire of the Holy Spirit to fall on me when I sat in that chair! I believe that their prayers along with others that the Lord had raised up helped open a door in my life so that I could move into listening prayer. I had developed a tremendous unbelief toward myself and I believed that I was just too ordinary for the Lord to speak to me in prayer.

I am thankful the Lord uses people despite ways that they struggle in their faith. Hebrews 11 clearly states that faith pleases God and that it is impossible to please God without faith:

> Now faith is confidence in what we hope for and assurance about what we do not see. [2] This is what the ancients were commended for.
>
> [6] And without faith it is impossible to please God, because anyone who comes to him must believe that he exists and that he rewards those who earnestly seek him. (Heb. 11:1-2, 6)

Through the prayers of others, the Lord in His mercy moved me from unbelief to faith. Your prayers for others matter, they really do!

In Acts 12, King Herod had James the brother of John put to death by the sword. This turned out to be a politically expedient move so then Peter was arrested, put in prison, and waiting to go on trial. Four squadrons of soldiers were guarding Peter and he slept chained to two soldiers. Meanwhile, a group was gathered at the house of John Mark's mother interceding in prayer for Peter. The intensity of that prayer meeting must have been incredible. Rest assured that they had cried out to the Holy Spirit to show them what to pray for Peter. Suddenly an angel appeared to Peter, woke him up, and loosed him from his chains. The angel walked him right by the rest of the soldiers, who were executed later because of Peter's escape. Peter wondered if he was merely having a vision, but after the angel left, he realized that the Lord had set him free. Peter showed up at the house where they were interceding. Rhoda, the servant girl, was so excited to see Peter that she forgot to let him in. She ran back to tell the others, and they didn't believe that Peter was really there.

I love that this detail that they didn't believe that Peter was there was included in the Bible. Unbelief is an ongoing battle that human beings deal with. When the Lord supernaturally released Peter, his intercessors had trouble believing that what they had been praying for had happened. The writers of scripture were committed to telling the truth rather than trying to make everyone think of them as spiritual giants. This humility speaks to the genuineness and authenticity of the Word of God. In spite of our doubts, God in His mercy can still use us to intercede for others. If you are hungry to move into listening prayer, but you find yourself plagued with doubt about the ministry of the Holy Spirit, there is hope. I will be sharing more in a later chapter about moving into victory over the doubt we have toward ourselves and toward the Lord. There is no way to fully describe the joy of partnering with the Holy Spirit to bless others by doing listening prayer on their behalf. So why let doubt hinder you from moving into listening to the Lord in prayer on behalf of others?

Listen: Adventures Await

Listening prayer also opens the door for us to go on adventures with Jesus. Jesus used the metaphor of sheep with a shepherd to describe what our relationship with Him could look like, should we choose to make Him the leader of our lives:

> The thief comes to kill, steal, and destroy, but I have come that you might have life, that it might be full and meaningful. (John 10:10 AMP)

> My sheep listen to my Voice, I know them, and they follow me. (John 10:27 NIV)

In the year 2000, I received in prayer that an important assignment that the Lord had for me was to help with revival on university and college campuses. The revelation was so intense that I knew that was one of the reasons that I had been born. I thought about this word from the Lord continually: "Lord, when I am going to begin this assignment. I'm getting older by the minute, Lord, but I trust You even though I don't understand." Yet, all I seemed to be doing was waiting. In 2006, Coach Tag and Pastor David heard in prayer for me, "Delay is not denial," on back-to-back days. At the time, I thought the message had to do with getting a job. However, I discovered later that this word from the Lord had more than one meaning. "Delay is not denial" had to do with the heaviest assignment on my heart: the college revival assignment. But still, all I did was wait. I guess I pictured standing on a platform somewhere preaching, but the truth was that I just didn't know what this assignment from the Lord was all about. Finally, in March of 2016, I received in prayer to start visiting university and college campuses across the nation to pray for revival. One day, as I was praying on one of the many campuses I've visited, I heard in prayer that this was what the Lord was talking to me about way back in 2000. All of this is to say that God has all kind of adventures for us to go on if we will say yes to whatever He directs. I wonder, what are the adventures that Jesus has for you to go on as you follow Him by listening to His voice?

Listen: Above All, Love

Finally, listening prayer helps us experience the love of Jesus as well as share the love of Jesus with others. Many people question whether or not they are loved. One of Satan's favorite tactics is to manipulate situations so that people get abused and rejected and then Satan will to try to get people to blame God for what happened. Satan loves to plant doubt in people so that they will turn away from the Lord: "How could God actually love you if this is what happened to you?"

Tommy was at the nurses' Bible study helping us pray. Listen to what happened when Tommy prayed for one of the nurses:

Wedding prayer

"One of the most wild prayers I prayed was while I was having an incredibly difficult night. A few of us were praying for the nurses and I prayed for a nurse that I had never met before. I had no idea that she was having a difficult time. The two main things I prayed was that God was going to

put a ring on her finger that she didn't have to take off and He was going to put a wedding dress on her that she didn't have to take off. What I didn't know is that a few months earlier she was engaged and the man she was engaged to broke things off and she was heartbroken. She had her wedding dress in a box in her closet."

Now this nurse is married and remembers how God and Jesus made their love known to her during this powerful time of receiving listening prayer.

Now, listen to Jesus' words from the book of Revelation: "Here I am! I stand at the door and knock. If anyone hears my voice and opens the door, I will come in and eat with that person, and they with me" (3:20).

When I first moved into listening prayer, I was shocked at how often the Lord told me that He loved me. The Holy Spirit loves to make the love of Jesus known to our hearts! The intimacy and fellowship with Jesus that have been made available to us through listening prayer is incredible. Do you long to have a closer relationship with Jesus? Why not step into the closeness with Jesus that your heart is longing for?

When we make listening prayer about the love of Jesus, we stay on track. But if we are not careful, we can begin to think that listening prayer is about the one doing the praying instead of the One that is the author of the prayer. When pride comes into the picture, listening prayer becomes something that it was never intended to be. Paul encouraged the church at Corinth to pursue spiritual gifts with passion. Paul told them to eagerly desire the gifts of the Spirit, but especially prophesy (1 Cor. 14:1). But Paul wanted the Corinthians to understand the context for the use of spiritual gifts. Unless these gifts were accompanied by the love of Jesus, the gifts accomplished nothing.

We have prayed for thousands of college and university students. It is not uncommon to see someone burst into tears as they are being prayed for. Having experienced this emotion myself the first time someone prayed for me with listening prayer, I can say you weep because you are overwhelmed with the realization of how much the Lord loves you. Many struggle with learning to listen in prayer due to the leap of faith that it often requires. You may receive words or a vision in prayer, but your mind may then make judgments, such as "You would have to be stupid to pray something like that!" But you have to know that the Lord loves to love on people when we are willing to put ourselves out there and feel uncomfortable. So, even though you feel like you are like that shaky new skater, and out there on thin ice, you take the risk of faith and pray with boldness what you are receiving, knowing that the Holy Spirit wants to reveal the incredible love of Jesus to people.

You have no idea how much I needed to hear that

Aaron has learned to risk loving on people by praying for people at his job. One day a patient came in to receive some tests from Aaron. In Aaron's own words: "A patient came in who 'looked the part.' He was maybe fifty years old and had lived quite the life. I specifically heard the Lord tell me, 'Say that I love him so much.' That was the last thing that I wanted to say to this tattooed, rather large, Harley Davidson-looking fellow. To me that sounded more like a bumper sticker you see on the back of a car. So, I approached him and said, 'Hey man, I feel like God has put it on my heart to tell you that He loves you so much.' He paused, and then looked at me and said, 'You have no idea how much I needed to hear that.' He asked if he could hug me! I hesitantly said, 'Sure.' Turns out that he was a meth addict and had been struggling with drugs for years. He spent some time in prison when he was younger due to grand theft auto. He told me his mom was a Christian and that he had good memories of her talking about the Lord. I ended up seeing him one week later as he was being discharged from the hospital and we exchanged numbers. He said, 'You were one of the first people I saw when I came in here and now the last.' We kept in touch. He ended up coming to church and getting baptized, rededicating his life to the Lord. This experience really enlightened me to the fact that it's not about how much you say, but it's about being in the Holy Spirit."

علم

The love of God is so amazing, it really is! The cross of Jesus came straight from the heart of God. Jesus, God's beloved Son, suffered incredible pain on the cross so that we could know that we can be forgiven. The Apostle Paul referred to himself as the chief of sinners because of his role in persecuting the early church. The love of God was real to Paul. After Paul encountered the risen Christ on the Damascus Road, no one needed to convince him that he was a sinner in need of a Savior. Listen to what Paul said about how the love of God made reconciliation with God possible because of the cross of Jesus:

> [6] You see, at just the right time, when we were still powerless, Christ died for the ungodly. [7] Very rarely will anyone die for a righteous person, though for a good person someone might possibly dare to die. [8] But God demonstrates his own love for us in this: While we were still sinners, Christ died for us. (Rom. 5:6-8)

But when you hate yourself, it is difficult to believe that God could really love you. Many people suffer from deep rejection. Many have been through situations that make them believe that God could never love them. "If God really loved me, I would have never gone through what I did." Satan loves this particular lie because it can keep someone separated from the love of God for years. Others have done things that make them believe that it's too late to come home to the Lord. The shame that they live with keeps them from approaching our holy God. But the Lord in his mercy has provided a way for the amazing truth of the love of God to become a reality in our lives as revealed in the cross of Jesus: "And hope does not put us to shame, because God's love has been poured out into our hearts through the Holy Spirit, who has been given to us" (Rom. 5:5).

If you will, the Holy Spirit takes the love of God made possible for us in the cross of Jesus and downloads this love right into our hearts. Three of us were walking onto a university campus and I was explaining to the guy who was going out with us for the first time that sometimes people burst into tears because of how loved Jesus makes them feel. The first person that I prayed for burst into tears and said, "You have no idea how much I needed this today!" The three of us were moved by how the love of Jesus was being poured out on this awesome college student through the simple act of listening prayer.

Of course it's not only college students who need listening prayer. Listen to my story about Nelson.

It was just what I needed

I first met Nelson when I shared a couple of talks on listening prayer at the church that he attended. Nelson is a retired engineer who loves the Lord and wants to make an impact for the Kingdom of God in his retirement years. After we met, it was obvious that the Lord had been setting him up for years to move into listening prayer. Not only did Nelson begin practicing listening prayer, but he and I worked on a listening prayer course for his local church for about six months. One day Nelson was taking some family members out for dinner. When it came time to the leave the tip, the Lord started speaking to him. The tip amount he got in prayer was much higher than he had anticipated. Indeed, it was more than the total bill for the meals. As they were leaving, the server ran after them to thank them and shared that she had been in a really tough place financially and that the tip that he had left was just the right amount that she needed to get past the situation she was in.

Listening to the Lord in prayer is awesome. You know that you want to move into listening prayer, don't you!

When we encounter the incredible love of God through the Holy Spirit, we can't help but think that we don't deserve this kind of love being poured out on us. It's the kindness of the Lord that leads us to repentance: "Or do you show contempt for the riches of his kindness, forbearance and patience, not realizing that God's kindness is intended to lead you to repentance?" (Rom. 2:4).

The love of Jesus is so real. When we partner with the Holy Spirit, we get to see the love of Jesus being manifested in people's lives who formerly had no hope.

When we pray for people with listening prayer, our motivation for this ministry is the love of God. Paul said that it was the love of God that motivated his ministry: "For Christ's love compels us, because we are convinced that one died for all, and therefore all died. [15] And he died for all, that those who live should no longer live for themselves but for him who died for them and was raised again" (2 Cor. 5:14-15). An important goal in listening prayer is that people will experience the love of God and the holiness of God up close and personal. Through the ministry of the Holy Spirit, we are inviting people to become forgiven followers of the Lord Jesus Christ!

The love of Jesus has to be the motivation for listening prayer if we want to pave the way for the love of God to be poured out into people's hearts through the Holy Spirit. Paul spoke the truth in love to the Corinthian church about what the true motivation for their ministries needed to be. Spiritual pride was a serious issue for this church. If listening prayer is done with an attitude rooted in spiritual pride, the work of the Holy Spirit is quenched. We must keep these Holy Spirit-inspired words at the heart of everything that we do in listening prayer:

> If I speak in the tongues of men or of angels, but do not have love, I am only a resounding gong or a clanging cymbal. [2] If I have the gift of prophecy and can fathom all mysteries and all knowledge, and if I have a faith that can move mountains, but do not have love, I am nothing. [3] If I give all I possess to the poor and give over my body to hardship that I may boast, but do not have love, I gain nothing.
>
> [4] Love is patient, love is kind. It does not envy, it does not boast, it is not proud. [5] It does not dishonor others, it is not self-seeking, it is not easily angered, it keeps no record of wrongs. [6] Love does not delight in evil but rejoices with the truth. [7] It always protects, always trusts, always hopes, always perseveres. (1 Cor. 13:1-7)

I will never forget praying for a pastor in an airport. I prayed for him in a state of spiritual competitiveness rather than praying for him through the love of Christ. Later that day when I realized what I had done, I was so disappointed in myself that I had actually done that to another pastor. Paul originally spoke this to the Corinthian church, but it was the Word of the Lord to me that day as well: "Brothers and sisters, I could not address you as people who live by the Spirit but as people who are still worldly—mere infants in Christ" (1 Cor. 3:1)

But before you judge me, please realize that all of us are susceptible to praying from a place of pride. If we begin to think that we are incapable of using holy things like prayer in worldly ways, we set ourselves up for a fall. Everything that we do in listening prayer has been made possible because of the grace of God.

Here is the attitude that we need when we approach listening to the Lord in prayer: "[1] Therefore, be imitators of God as dearly loved children [2] and live in love, just as Christ also loved us and gave himself for us, a sacrificial and fragrant offering to God" (Eph. 5:1-2 NET).

Listening prayer is like being a little kid who gets to watch Jesus give another little kid a new bike at Christmas. Listening prayer gives us the rare privilege of being on the front row and watching the Lord surprise someone with the love of Jesus.

As you study the Word of God, you will probably come up with other incredible motivations to learn to listen to the Lord in prayer in addition the ones I've mentioned here. But I've mentioned these to try to inspire you to say yes to whatever the Lord wants to do in your life. Why not say to the Lord that the longing of your heart is to know Him and to learn to listen to His voice in prayer?

> *Dear Lord, I pray that You would be honored and glorified through my life. I pray, Lord, that You would teach me to be led by the Holy Spirit as I pray so that people know how much You love them. I ask to hear Your voice in prayer, Lord, so that I can pray for people to help them to come to know Jesus as the Son of God. In Jesus' name, I pray. Amen.*

CHAPTER 3

How God Speaks

One day at our campus ministry at Florida State University, a woman came and prayed for some of the students with whom I worked on almost a daily basis. I was stunned at her prayers. To say that I was astonished doesn't even come close to my reaction observing the Lord love these students through what I knew to be personalized, specific words in her prayers. I was filled with so many questions. I thought, how in the world do you move into knowing the Lord like this? Later, sitting on the edge of the stage, I felt discouraged. I thought, "I know how to do campus ministry but I am so ill-equipped to do a ministry like this." As I sat there, I thought about three or four other things that I was upset about. A young woman named Esi, a freshman from Ghana, came over to me and said, "Pastor, the Lord told me to come and sit by you." The first question that came to my mind was how did the Lord speak to you? The second question was how did you know for sure it was the Lord? But instead of asking any questions, I said, "Since you are here, why don't you go ahead and pray for me." This is how her prayer started: "Thank you, Lord, that even though Pastor feels ill equipped to do this ministry, I thank you that you are going to equip him with everything that he needs." The rest of her prayer spoke word-for-word to what I had just been upset about in the exact order that I had just thought it. I took Esi over to the amazing prayer warrior that had been praying for our group and asked them both to pray that what the Lord was doing in their lives would also happen in mine.

When most people hear the phrase "God speaking," they can't help but think of God speaking in an audible voice. While God does speak audibly at times, it is not the only way that He speaks. In this chapter, we'll look at a few different ways He might speak to you.

God Speaks: The Audible Voice

There are many biblical examples of God speaking in an audible voice. Here is one story, in which not just a single person heard his voice, but many did at once:

> 27 "Now my soul is deeply troubled. Should I pray, 'Father, save me from this hour'? But this is the very reason I came! 28 Father, bring glory to your name." Then a voice spoke from heaven, saying, "I have already brought glory to my name, and I will do so again." 29 When the crowd heard the voice, some thought it was thunder, while others declared an angel had spoken to him.
>
> 30 Then Jesus told them, "The voice for your benefit, not mine." (John 12:27-30 NIV)

Just as He is recorded to have spoken in the past, God still speaks in an audible voice today. I have not had the privilege of hearing from the Lord in this way, but know others who have. Listen to Lena's story:

Rescued by the audible voice of God

Lena almost didn't make it here. Her mother had been exposed to incredible spiritual darkness growing up and had some serious health issues. Because of the intensity of the medications she was taking, pregnancy was not an option. So when she found out she was pregnant, she was told to schedule an abortion. His wife's doctors told Lena's dad about the upcoming abortion as if it was a done deal. He began to pour himself into his farming work even more intensely than usual, trying to escape the pain of the situation. To his total surprise, God spoke to him in an audible voice. The Lord told him that the baby needed to be born and that she had a call of revival on her life. Against all medical advice, Lena's dad checked his wife out of the hospital. He found a Christian doctor who understood the serious concerns about continuing the pregnancy, but was willing to help them. Lena was supposed to be born with all kinds of deformities, but instead she was born a month early, a happy, healthy baby.

When Lena was 13 she went on a mission trip to Canada with her church. She began to experience the reality of the Lord's voice even though doing so would have been unusual in her church. On the trip, she saw some of the people that she prayed for before the meetings get saved. She saw people who felt sick or had migraines before ministry time get healed through her prayers. An influential friend gave her a backpack that she had used on one of her mission trips. Lena would often hold this backpack when she prayed. The Lord spoke to her heart that she would be going to Africa the next year. She asked her parents if she raised the money to go on a mission trip to Africa, could she have their word that they would let her go. They said yes, thinking there was no way that she could ever raise the money. Lena raised twice the amount needed to go on the mission trip through selling candy bars and making meals. She was even able to help some of the other members of the team with their finances. At 14, Lena went to Africa on a short-term mission trip.

Today, Lena is in her twenties and has a huge heart for revival. The Lord spoke to Lena's dad about her future; the Lord spoke to Lena. Their examples show that hearing His voice and following His word lead to fulfillment of Kingdom purposes.

God Speaks: Angels

In Acts, we read about great revival in Samaria. In the midst of people being healed, saved, and delivered, listen to how the Lord communicated His will to Phillip for his next assignment:

> 26 As for Philip, an angel of the Lord said to him, "Go south down the desert road that runs from Jerusalem to Gaza." 27 So he started out, and he met the treasurer of Ethiopia, a eunuch of great authority under the Kandake, the queen of Ethiopia. The eunuch had gone to Jerusalem to worship, 28 and he was now returning. Seated in his carriage, he was reading aloud from the book of the prophet Isaiah.
>
> 29 The Holy Spirit said to Philip, "Go over and walk along beside the carriage." (Acts 8:26-29)

In the midst of a mighty revival, an angel told Philip to go to a desert place for one person. The Lord communicated His will first through an angel and then, through the Holy Spirit, He gave Philip further direction. We don't know if the Holy Spirit spoke in an audible voice or communicated directly to Phillip's heart. We also don't know if the angel appeared in response to prayer. It would seem, though, that as we continue to seek the Lord the way that the Ethiopian eunuch did, we open the door for more and more communication from the Lord.

The philosopher Blaise Pascal was asked why the Lord didn't reveal Himself to people in such a way that they wouldn't be able to doubt His existence. Pascal responded that God keeps Himself partially hidden so that if we want to find Him we will, and if we don't want to find Him, we won't. God in His mercy sometimes reveals Himself to people that are not even seeking Him. But we should never presume on the Lord's mercy for this. Listen to this admonition.

> [11] For I know the plans I have for you," declares the LORD, "plans to prosper you and not to harm you, plans to give you hope and a future. [12] Then you will call on me and come and pray to me, and I will listen to you. [13] You will seek me and find me when you seek me with all your heart. (Jer. 29:11-13)

Remember Brother Harold, who through the listening prayer of a friend escaped being shot by bow and arrow? He walked away from an incredible job at the Department of Education in the state of Florida in the 1980s to radically pursue following Jesus wherever He might lead. Before Brother Harold died, he had traveled to over 65 nations on assignment from the Lord. After Brother Harold stepped away from his job, he attended a ministry school. One morning, a number of people were seeking the Lord in prayer during a time of personal worship and prayer in the small chapel at the school. Suddenly, Brother Harold saw a large angel standing at the front of the chapel writing on a tablet. Brother Harold went up to the angel and asked what he was doing. The angel told him that he was writing down assignments from the Lord for the people in the room. As you can imagine, this experience inspired Brother Harold to seek the Lord's assignments for his life with great intensity.

On another occasion, Brother Harold and his wife Nancy were in a group that was on a tour of the Upper Room in

Jerusalem. The Lord allowed both Brother Harold and Nancy to see angels walking around the room giving gifts to people. As with Philip in the Bible, as with Brother Harold and Nancy, and countless others, the Lord may speak to you through an angel, allowing you to receive instructions from the Lord.

God Speaks: Visions

In Acts 16, Paul received a vision of a man from Macedonia begging for help:

> [6] Next Paul and Silas traveled through the area of Phrygia and Galatia, because the Holy Spirit had prevented them from preaching the word in the province of Asia at that time. [7] Then coming to the borders of Mysia, they headed north for the province of Bithynia, but again the Spirit of Jesus did not allow them to go there. [8] So instead, they went on through Mysia to the seaport of Troas.
>
> [9] That night Paul had a vision: A man from Macedonia in northern Greece was standing there, pleading with him, "Come over to Macedonia and help us!" [10] So we decided to leave for Macedonia at once, having concluded that God was calling us to preach the Good News there. (Acts 16:6-10)

The whole world needs the gospel of Jesus! Paul had a heart to take the gospel to the world. But where do we start, we wonder, and does God really have strategic plans for our lives, and what would it be like to receive direction from Him for our ministries? In Acts 16, although we don't know the exact manner through which the Holy Spirit communicated, we see the Holy Spirit stopped Paul from going to certain places. After the Holy Spirit prevented Paul from going to Asia and Bithynia, Paul was given a vision of a man begging them to come to Macedonia. The vision let Paul know where to go next to share the gospel. This vision from the Lord would ultimately lead to the beginning of the Philippian church.

As I shared earlier, Brother Harold had quit his job and was seeking God with all his heart asking what his assignments were for the sake of the Kingdom. On the day after a three-day fast, Brother Harold was on a plane and the Holy Spirit spoke to his heart to close his eyes. He closed his eyes, and saw an angel of fire walk down the aisle of the plane and stop at his seat. First, the angel led them to a burning bush, then a mountaintop where he was told to teach, preach, and heal. Next he was on a platform, preaching, healing, and doing deliverance in front of people all dressed in white. Then, he was in a boat enclosed in the light of the Holy Spirit, then an airplane, and then in a two-wheeled cart being pulled by an animal in a bright light. Last, he saw the Lamb of God on a throne with blood on Him. This scene changed to Jesus on the cross, then to Jesus in the powerful form from the book of Revelation. Finally, just for emphasis, Brother Harold had a dream that was exactly the same as the vision. All these things that God spoke to him through visions and dreams came to pass in Brother Harold's ministry. The book *In His Service* tells the story of how these and other dreams and visions that Brother Harold received in prayer were fulfilled in his ministry.

Listen now to Rob's story.

Seeing Jesus

My friend Rob found himself terrified to wake up every day. He had health problems, had lost his job, and was heavily addicted to drugs and alcohol. For two months Rob had been thinking about appearing before God without much to show for his life. Finally, after listening to a Billy Graham video, he gave his life to Christ. When the video first started, Billy Graham was saying that people needed to repent of their sins and then to believe in Jesus to be born again. Rob almost dismissed this because he thought about how he'd heard that repentance thing his whole life and how it doesn't work. What Billy Graham said next got Rob's attention. Billy said, "Some of you might not have the power to repent so you can ask the Lord for the power to repent." Rob did just that. Suddenly Rob saw Jesus from the neck up, lit up like stars. He was smiling with his mouth wide open. Almost two months later, Rob saw an open vision of Jesus on the cross. At the vision, Rob cried. He had never cried like that before. He wept and wept. Four days later, Rob had a vision of going down a tunnel. He ended up at a sewer grate with fire flashing beneath it. He saw shadows of people moving and he cried out, "Lord, take me back." Rob then heard the audible voice of the Lord telling him to read Psalm 18 and Psalm 118 and He also gave Rob a couple of commands to carry out. When Rob woke up the next morning after hearing the Lord's audible voice, he was completely healed of a bad hip, a bad back, and a crooked neck.

One evening I was with a group of college students who were praying for each other. In times of listening prayer like this, I have seen Jesus do tremendous healing in people's hearts. At the beginning of Jesus' ministry, He quoted a passage from Isaiah that prophesied what His ministry was going to look like.

> [16] So He came to Nazareth, where He had been brought up. And as His custom was, He went into the synagogue on the Sabbath day, and stood up to read. [17] And He was handed the book of the prophet Isaiah. And when He had opened the book, He found the place where it was written:
>
> [18] "The Spirit of the LORD *is* upon Me,
> Because He has anointed Me

To preach the gospel to *the* poor;
He has sent Me to heal the brokenhearted,
To proclaim liberty to *the* captives
And recovery of sight to *the* blind,
To set at liberty those who are oppressed;
[19] To proclaim the acceptable year of the LORD."

[20] Then He closed the book, and gave *it* back to the attendant and sat down. And the eyes of all who were in the synagogue were fixed on Him. [21] And He began to say to them, "Today this Scripture is fulfilled in your hearing." (Luke 4:18 NKJV)

It is incredible that now through the Holy Spirit we can continue what Jesus began to do and to teach (Acts 1:1-5).

A shattered heart healed

One evening at a student gathering we saw a student receive healing for her broken heart through listening prayer. One person praying for her saw her in a garden as a little girl and Jesus picking her up in His arms. We found out that when she was in the 9th grade, her parents divorced. When she prayed, she would always go to a place in her mind where she was a little girl in a garden being picked up by Jesus. Another person saw a picture of a glass heart that had lots of cracks in it that was being put back together again. Five separate people came over to her and quoted Zephaniah 3:17: "The Lord your God is with you, the Mighty Warrior who saves. He will take great delight in you; in His love He will no longer rebuke you, but will rejoice over you with singing." A sixth person sang over her as a mom would sing over a child. Jesus continues to heal the brokenhearted through the leading of the Holy Spirit in listening prayer!

God Speaks: Dreams

God speaks in dreams. Here is an example from the New Testament of an incredibly famous dream:

> [19] Joseph, to whom Mary was engaged, was a righteous man and did not want to disgrace her publicly, so he decided to break the engagement quietly.
>
> [20] As he considered this, an angel of the Lord appeared to him in a dream. "Joseph, son of David," the angel said, "do not be afraid to take Mary as your wife. For the child within her was conceived by the Holy Spirit.
>
> [21] And she will have a son, and you are to name him Jesus, for he will save his people from their sins." (Matt. 1:20-21)

Those of you who constantly attend meetings have my utmost respect. I have to fight becoming mildly annoyed even after good meetings, so hats off to you folks who go from one meeting to the next. One day, having attended hour upon hour of meetings, I was thinking, "You can't be serious, when will this be over?" After all the meetings, I set the noble goal of straightening up my office. In the midst of my office rearranging, I stopped and said, "This is ridiculous; I'm sorry Lord, what should I do the rest of the afternoon?" I am so glad that I laid my bad attitude down that day and began to listen in prayer. Instead of straightening up my office, I had an experience that I will never forget for the rest of my life because I listened in prayer.

As I moved into listening prayer that day, I heard on the inside, "Go on a prayer drive." In the middle of my prayer drive, I heard again on the inside, "Call Brother Harold." Brother Harold's wife Nancy answered the phone and I said, "I got in prayer to call Brother Harold and I don't know why." She said, "Of course you did. Brother Harold got in prayer this morning to pack his bags because it was time to come home to the Lord." A day and a half later, Brother Harold died. Nancy said it was like being on holy ground as Brother Harold approached death. The afternoon that I finally stopped and listened to the Lord, the afternoon that I got in prayer to call Brother Harold instead of straightening up my office, was the last time that I received prayer from Brother Harold before he died. I hadn't known how sick he had been up to that point because whenever I called he was so busy mentoring me he never mentioned his failing health. I almost missed that last phone call because my plan was to straighten up my office.

Thankfully, I had stopped what I was doing and had asked the Lord for His daily assignment for me. Nancy told me that on the last day of Brother Harold's life, he was still listening to the Lord and doing the Lord's ministry. Early in the morning of Brother Harold's last day on earth, he was awakened with a dream from the Lord. He had a dream about a missionary couple that he hadn't talked to in over five years. Brother Harold got Nancy to place the call and then he shared the dream that he had received with this couple even though he could barely talk. When Nancy got on the phone with the couple, they were crying. They shared that life had been so hard that they had started to wonder if they were still even Christians. They said that Brother Harold's dream had meant everything to them. A couple of hours later, Brother Harold died and got to see Jesus face-to-face and join the great cloud of witnesses in his heavenly home. Years earlier I had prayed earnestly, "Lord, please put someone in my life that can teach me how to know Jesus in a deeper way and how to walk in the Spirit." The Lord answered my prayer by putting Brother Harold in my life.

When I first encountered listening prayer, the whole thing baffled me because I had no idea how it worked, and I had no idea how to listen to God speak. This chapter is a result of the hours that I spent searching the scriptures trying to grasp how the ministry of the Holy Spirit works. The Lord increased my hunger to know Him by making it possible to spend time with

Brother Harold. Brother Harold taught me to be dependent on the Holy Spirit rather than on him. So much of what I am sharing in this book comes from listening to the Lord in prayer. The Holy Spirit will be your teacher if you ask Him to. Brother Harold taught me through the way that he lived his life that the best dreams to live out are the dreams that the Lord has for our lives. Brother Harold was living for the Lord instead of for himself even on the last day of his life. I thank God for the witness of Brother Harold.

God Speaks: Words in Our Hearts

Eventually, after crying out for the Lord to speak to me over a two-year period, I began to receive words in my heart in prayer. A passage from 1 Corinthians 2 helped me understand how the Holy Spirit leads us in prayer:

> [9] However, as it is written:

> "What no eye has seen,
> what no ear has heard,
> and what no human mind has conceived"—
> the things God has prepared for those who love
> him—

> [10] these are the things God has revealed to us by his Spirit.

> The Spirit searches all things, even the deep things of God. [11] For who knows a person's thoughts except their own spirit within them? In the same way no one knows the thoughts of God except the Spirit of God. [12] What we have received is not the spirit of the world, but the Spirit who is from God, so that we may understand what God has freely given us. [13] This is what we speak, not in words taught us by human wisdom but in words taught by the Spirit, explaining

spiritual realities with Spirit-taught words.
(1 Cor. 2:9-13)

In the first month of learning to listen to the Lord in prayer, the Lord did some things for me that showed me how real listening to God is. Years earlier at a funeral, I told a story about giving this man a simple prayer to pray before he died. I told him that this prayer has been prayed for centuries. This is the prayer: "Lord Jesus Christ, Son of God, have mercy on me a sinner." After the funeral, the man's son said that we needed to talk about that prayer sometime. Five years later, his daughter was preparing for a bone marrow transplant. I asked for three nights in a row to come pray for her. He said that he was really sorry but that she was too sick to see anyone. The third night he told me that they were headed to a hospital in Gainesville, Florida the next day.

The very next day I was in a hospital in Tallahassee, Florida. I had just finished praying my first listening prayer for a patient there. As I walked out of the hospital room, I heard on the inside: stop, turn left, walk. I was beyond excited! I remembered a student had given this scripture to me previously and said that it was for my life: "[21] Whether you turn to the right or to the left, your ears will hear a voice behind you, saying, 'This is the way; walk in it'" (Isa. 30:21).

What was happening had my full attention. Next I heard: stop, turn right, walk! Now I was walking down another hallway in complete amazement. I heard to turn left. I saw an exit sign and a stairwell and began to wonder what was on the other floor. The next thing I knew, I had walked into someone's hospital room. The girl that was supposed to be three hours away in a Gainesville hospital was in that very room in Tallahassee! I talked to her grandmother who was as shocked as I was when I told her how I got there. I was there just long enough to pray for her granddaughter before the staff came and got her for some tests.

The second experience in that first month of learning to listen to the Lord happened at a friend's church. I had been asked to pray for the youth director. In the middle of the prayer, I heard on the inside to pray: "Every night of your life you think you are going to die. I break this lie in Jesus' name." On the inside I said, "Lord, I can't pray that. That is either true or it's not." Again, I heard, "Say it!" and I said on the inside; "I just can't say this!" I objected three times and then I finally said it. When I finished the prayer, the youth director started running around the room saying, "It's gone, it's gone!" He came up to me, grabbed my shoulders, and said, "Every night of my life I sit in a chair and think I'm going to die of a heart attack. It's gone; it's gone!" For about twenty minutes on the way home I kept saying over and over to the Lord: "Lord, that was impressive. I mean, really, wow, that was impressive Lord! Seriously, Lord, That Was Impressive!!!"

Some people believe that the Holy Spirit stopped speaking after the age of the apostles. While I never thought the Holy Spirit stopped speaking, I did have a hard time believing that the Lord would speak to me because I am so ordinary. I believed that God could part the Red Sea, but somehow, I also believed that He was unable to speak to me. I knew that I was a sinner saved by grace, that my eternal salvation had been secured by asking Jesus to forgive me of my sins, and by asking Him to be the leader of my life. However, I still assumed that since I was a sinner the Lord couldn't use someone like me. My logic was incredibly flawed. If the Lord could only use perfect people, then the only one that He could ever use would be Jesus. The two all-stars of the New Testament are Peter and Paul. Peter denied Jesus and Paul referred to himself as the chief of sinners because of orchestrating the deaths of some of the early Jesus followers. Here is the good news: the Lord longs for a deep, personal relationship with people. After all, He made us in His image. Because of Jesus' death and resurrection, the Lord has made possible incredible intimacy with Him if we will but say yes to His offer of salvation and Kingdom of God purposes for our lives! Why miss this?

¹⁴"Therefore, since we have a great high priest who has gone through the heavens, Jesus the Son of God, let us hold firmly to the faith we profess. ¹⁵For we do not have a high priest who is unable to sympathize with our weaknesses, but we have one who has been tempted in every way, just as we are—yet was without sin. ¹⁶Let us then approach the throne of grace with confidence, so that we may receive mercy and find grace to help us in our time of need." (Heb. 4:14-16)

So why waste another day in pointless activity? Why not step into your Kingdom of God destiny? If you doubt yourself the way that I did, I can assure you, there is hope for you. I encourage you to make yourself available to God and say to Him that you are willing for Him to do in your life whatever He wants to do. Tell him that you will follow Jesus anywhere and that you want to live for Him rather than for yourself. Ask Him to speak to you. He will!

Dear Lord, I confess that I have a hard time believing that You would want to speak to someone like me, so I have never even considered that listening prayer could ever be a part of my life and ministry for You. Forgive me for my unbelief. I am willing, Lord, for You to do in my life whatever You want to do. In Jesus' name, I pray. Amen.

CHAPTER 4

The Heart of the Matter

The condition of the heart is essential to listening prayer. When the heart is not right, everything can go south in a hurry. But when the heart is in great condition, health and life flow in great freedom. Kim, an intercessor I know, once shared with me that while she was interceding for someone, the Lord allowed her to see the condition of that person's heart. She saw blood flowing freely through the person's heart: no blockages restricted its flow. Not only was the person's own blood flowing, but Kim also saw the blood of Jesus flowing through the heart. She explained that because of the depth of surrender to the Lord that this person had gone through, all blockages had been removed. Without blockages, the person received much from the Lord in prayer. What Kim saw in picture form, the Lord has shown me is of the utmost importance if we are to move into hearing from Him. We need to come before the Lord with hearts open, gentle, and humble like Jesus', which allows His blood to flow through our hearts.

Maybe you have been wondering why I am taking so long to explain how we are activated into hearing from the Lord. This is the issue: the difficulty with moving into hearing from the Lord is not a cognitive issue; it is a heart issue. I have seen children move quickly into hearing from the Lord because they don't have years of unbelief and other heart issues adults must wade through. The realization we need to see is that hearing from the Lord becomes challenging because of the condition of our hearts. Blockages in our hearts prevent us from being able to receive from the Lord. I call the state we need to be in to receive in prayer *whatever* mode. We have to learn how to get into whatever mode so that we truly are open to whatever the Lord wants to say to us or direct us to do for the sake of His Kingdom.

In the gospel of Matthew, Jesus teaches us about the importance of the condition of our hearts. We learn through the Beatitudes that if our hearts are pure, we will be able to see God (Matt. 5:8). Jesus tells us to take His yoke upon us because He is gentle and humble of heart (Matt. 11:29). We are to love the Lord our God with all of our hearts and with all of our souls and all of our minds (Matt. 22:37). When our hearts are set right, when they are pure and healthy, they are like fertile, well-cultivated soil, ready to bear fruit.

Identifying Damaged Hearts

But here is the problem: our hearts are not right. Even once set right, they are naturally prone to damage and decay if not properly cared for. What Jesus said about many of the people of His day can also be said about us: "These people honor me with their lips, but their hearts are far from me" (Matt. 15:8). Listen, too, to this rebuke from Jesus for the church at Ephesus, knowing full well we could often qualify for the same rebuke: "[4] Yet I hold this against you: You have forsaken the love you had at first. [5] Consider how far you have fallen! Repent and do the things you did at first" (Rev. 2:4-5).

King David, though known as a man after God's own heart, was far from perfect and subject to falling. In fact, to cover up the affair he had with Bathsheba, he arranged to have her husband

Uriah put on the front lines to be killed. But when the prophet Nathan confronted him, David did not respond with a prideful statement such as, "I am the king, who in the world do you think you are talking to!" Instead, David humbled himself before God. Listen to David's anguished cry after he realized what he had done had been not only a sin against Uriah and Bathsheba, but a sin against the Lord as well:

> 2 Wash away all my iniquity
>   and cleanse me from my sin.
> 3 For I know my transgressions,
>   and my sin is always before me.
> 4 Against you, you only, have I sinned
>   and done what is evil in your sight;
>   so you are right in your verdict
>   and justified when you judge.
> 10 Create in me a pure heart, O God,
>   and renew a steadfast spirit within me.
> (Psalm 51:2-4, 10)

David's sin set in motion a great deal of devastation. Because he was quick to repent and to humble himself before the Lord, the Lord was still able to use him. While David was known as a man whose heart was devoted to the Lord, his son Solomon was known by the Lord as a man whose heart had been turned away to other gods. Listen to what the Lord had to say about David and his son Solomon: "As Solomon grew old, his wives turned his heart after other gods, and his heart was not fully devoted to the Lord his God, as the heart of David his father had been" (1 Kings 11:4). God in His mercy will sometimes speak to people whose hearts are far from Him. However, when we presume on His grace, we set ourselves up to be lied to by the enemy's camp. If our desire is to draw close to the heart of God and to listen to the Lord in prayer, we need to ask the Lord to cleanse our hearts the way that David did.

Here is the truth of the matter: sometimes we appear to be

all in with the Lord on the outside and yet our hearts can be far from Him. Jesus confronted religious leaders of his day with this difficult truth. What's even more difficult? Sometimes, it applies to us as well:

> [25] Woe to you, teachers of the law and Pharisees, you hypocrites! You clean the outside of the cup and dish, but inside they are full of greed and self-indulgence. [26] Blind Pharisee! First clean the inside of the cup and dish, and then the outside also will be clean. (Matt. 23:25-26)

We are easily distracted by the world and all too often our focus is on impressing people rather than living to please God. Sadly, we can even begin to have idolatrous hearts that fall in love with our sins. Blaise Pascal's philosophy pointed to a God-shaped void in our hearts that can only be filled by God and His Son Jesus. Yet, even when that heart-void has been filled by God, we can be prone to wander. If our heart condition is wrong, what we hear from the Lord becomes distorted, or His word may not even come through at all, because it gets blocked by worldly, unhealthy plaque buildup. James 3 provides a picture of how God's wisdom can become replaced by worldly wisdom because of heart problems: "[14] However, if you have bitter jealousy and selfish ambition in your heart, then stop bragging and living in ways that deny the truth. [15] This is not the wisdom that comes down from above. Instead, it is from the earth, natural and demonic" (James 3:14-15 CEV).

When we start caring too much about what people think, things like jealousy and selfish ambition can sneak in and cause us to miss what the Lord wants to say to us. Once ambition and jealousy are allowed a place in our hearts, the wisdom from above can get tainted. Having the right heart when we approach the Lord in prayer is essential if we hope to receive the Lord's wisdom as we pray. Jesus told a parable that highlighted the importance of getting our hearts right before God as we approach the Lord in prayer. In this parable, Jesus taught us to lay down the judgment we have toward others before we pray. We also need to approach the Lord with humble hearts, appreciative that it is the Lord's mercy that makes a relationship with Him even possible:

> [9] To some who were confident of their own righteous-ness and looked down on everyone else, Jesus told this parable: [10] "Two men went up to the temple to pray, one a Pharisee and the other a tax collector. [11] The Pharisee stood by himself and prayed: 'God, I thank you that I am not like other people—robbers, evildoers, adulterers—or even like this tax collector. [12] I fast twice a week and give a tenth of all I get.'
>
> [13] "But the tax collector stood at a distance. He would not even look up to heaven, but beat his breast and said, 'God, have mercy on me, a sinner.'
>
> [14] "I tell you that this man, rather than the other, went home justified before God. For all those who exalt themselves will be humbled, and those who humble themselves will be exalted." (Luke 18:9-14)

All of us are sinners in need of a Savior in desperate need of the mercy that was made available to us through the cross of Jesus. Once we genuinely realize that our own righteousness couldn't get the job done in making things right with the Lord, it changes the way we approach prayer. We need to come before our holy God the way the second man in the parable came before the Lord, saying, "God be merciful to me a sinner."

Artery Blocker: Pride of Self-Sufficiency

Pride can shield us from recognizing the desperate condition of our hearts. The pride in the church in Laodicea blinded them to how desperate their situation was. Listen to this rebuke from

Jesus: "[17] After all, you say, 'I'm rich, and I've grown wealthy, and I don't need a thing.' You don't realize that you are miserable, pathetic, poor, blind, and naked" (Rev. 3:17). The good news is that Jesus has the solution for us when we succumb to self-sufficiency. Jesus' correction is a sign of how much He loves us. "[19] Those whom I love I rebuke and discipline. So be earnest and repent" (Rev. 3:19).

When the prophet Samuel was looking for someone to anoint as king, one of David's brothers appeared to be a much better candidate for the job than David did. But the Lord told Samuel that He doesn't look at the outside; He looks at the heart. Here is the difficulty: our hearts can be wrong and we can be oblivious to our true condition just like the church at Laodicea was. So how do we know the true condition of our hearts? We need the Holy Spirit to show us. But how can the Holy Spirit show us this if we haven't learned how to listen to His voice? Try asking the Lord to speak to your heart about things you need to repent of and watch what happens!

Heart Revival: Repentance

We go to great lengths to avoid repentance. Before someone receives Christ as his or her Lord and Savior, the cross is an offense. Before we say yes to our need for Jesus, our pride gets offended when we are told that we are sinners in need of a Savior. Once we realize our desperate need for forgiveness through the cross of Jesus, we marvel at how deceived we were. Yet even after we've received Christ, we can get offended again if we are shown that we still need to repent about something. But the good news here is Jesus knocks on the door of the hearts of believers, waiting to have fellowship with them by sharing His voice through the Holy Spirit if they will only repent: "[19] Those whom I love I rebuke and discipline. So be earnest and repent. [20] Here I am! I stand at the door and knock. If anyone hears my voice and opens the door, I will come in and eat with that person, and they with me" (Rev. 3:19-20).

A couple of my colleagues and I held a small clergy gathering in response to what the Lord was doing through the Brownsville revival in the mid-1990s. Our planning group felt like I was the one to deliver the repentance message to the pastors. In the message I preached, I personally repented for living far below who the Lord had called me to be in Christ. I confessed to having a worldly heart and that I had been lukewarm like the Christians in Laodicea. At the end of the message, I began to knock on the wooden pulpit. In the otherwise silent room, I knocked louder and louder and felt the Lord's leading to just keep knocking. The intensity of the convicting power of the Holy Spirit came down upon us. Suddenly, pastors began running to the front to repent before Jesus our King. The purity and holiness of God's presence that came down that day was amazing. These pastors were not too proud to admit that they had become lukewarm. How about you? Ask yourself: is there a deep repentance that you need to go through before the Lord? Then listen for the Lord's answer.

> 23 Examine me, God! Look at my heart!
> Put me to the test! Know my anxious thoughts!
> 24 Look to see if there is any idolatrous way in me,
> then lead me on the eternal path!
> (Psalm 139:23-24 CEV)

We might not bow down to wooden or stone idols but we are susceptible to idolatrous devotion in our hearts. We fall in love with the world rather than with the Lord. John has a strong warning:

> 15 Do not love the world [of sin that opposes God and His precepts], nor the things that are in the world. If anyone loves the world, the love of the Father is not in him. 16 For all that is in the world—the lust *and* sensual craving of the flesh and the lust *and* longing of the eyes and the boastful pride of life [pretentious

> confidence in one's resources or in the stability of earthly things]—these do not come from the Father, but are from the world. [17] The world is passing away, and with it its lusts [the shameful pursuits and ungodly longings]; but the one who does the will of God *and* carries out His purposes lives forever. (1 John 2:15-17 AMP)

We place our affection on things in the world and dedicate our passion and loyalty to serving these things above all else. We even make idols out of people. And what's worse, we can even crave that people will make idols out of us. So, enough is enough! It's time to ask the Lord to search our hearts and ask Him to remove every blockage that keeps us from receiving what the Holy Spirit wants to share with us.

Heart Repair: Ongoing Need for Repentance

John the Baptist told the people to produce fruit in keeping with repentance. Repentance is more than just momentarily feeling bad and feeling sorry for what we have done. Repentance is a change of heart and life: the goal is to make us more like Jesus. Repentance is absolutely key to moving us into hearing from the Lord because it is the primary antidote to the pride that wants to come in and take over our lives. It would be nice if we could repent one time and never have to do it again. However, there is no hiding the motives of our hearts from the Lord. Our cup might look bright and shiny on the outside to others, but the Lord knows the real story. John the Baptist said that Jesus must increase and that he must decrease. This sounds great in theory until we are faced with living it out. But, if we are serious about wanting to hear the Lord's voice, then we can expect the Lord's presence to be like a refining fire in our lives.

Listening Invokes Repentance

I was new in listening to the Lord in prayer. Dave and I were praying for people and the Lord was pouring out His love and encouragement through the things we were praying for students. At the end of one of the prayers that I prayed for a student, I realized that something felt off about what I was praying. I received in prayer to ask for confirmation about what I had just prayed. The student said that everything you prayed was so true except for the last thing. He said that is not true of my life. That was exactly the point where I felt like something was off. I stopped praying for people because I sensed something was wrong and I had no idea what the problem might be.

The next day I was seeking the Lord about what happened. I asked the Lord if I had really missed it with what I prayed, and I got a yes. I asked what had happened. This is what I heard on the inside: "You were showing off in front of your friend." Immediately the conviction was intense. I weakly asked what I should do. I received to go to Dave's house and apologize. I knocked on Dave's door and asked if we could talk. I told him that I had been under intense conviction about the fact that I had been showing off in front of him the previous night. He said that he didn't think I was showing off but I assured him that I was. After repenting, I walked away and the love of Jesus hit me hard. I experienced the truth of Revelation 3:19 up close and personal: "Those whom I love I rebuke and discipline. So be earnest, and repent."

Ready for Surgery

When we pray for someone, we are surgical instruments that the Holy Spirit uses to do surgery on someone's heart. We want to become like sterilized surgical instruments in the Lord's hand, so we need to ask the Lord to create clean hearts in us through the blood of Jesus. Sometimes we just jump in to listening prayer and hear quickly from the Lord, but there are other times we need to carefully prepare ourselves to come before the Lord. Think of the elaborate procedures undertaken to prepare the high priest to come into the holy of holies once a year. Because of the blood of Jesus, we have been given unlimited access to the Father. Even so, we still need to prepare our hearts as we come before our holy Lord in the mighty name of Jesus. If there are wounded places in our hearts, it can distort what the Lord wants to say to us through listening prayer.

From Untamed Hearts to Fruitful Gardens

As we move into listening to the Lord, He begins to work on our character. Whether we realize it or not, all of us desperately need the Lord's correction. You will find out that your heart can be like a wild, overgrown garden in need of cultivation and repair. Rocks and brambles need to be removed and weeds need to be pulled up at the roots. The good news is that the Lord is patient and will show us step-by-step how to move into all that He has for us.

As you move into listening prayer, the Holy Spirit will be your teacher. As we abide in Jesus, the Holy Spirit will begin to prune us so that we will be able to bear much fruit.

> [1] I am the true vine, and my Father is the gardener. [2] He cuts off every branch in me that bears no fruit, while every branch that does bear fruit he prunes so that it will be even more fruitful. [3] You are already clean because of the word I have spoken to you. [4] Remain in me, as I also remain in you. No branch can bear fruit by itself; it must remain in the vine. Neither can you bear fruit unless you remain in me. [5] I am the vine; you are the branches. If you remain in me and I in you, you will bear much fruit; apart from me you can do nothing. (John 15:1-5)

I remember reading this Scripture passage one day and thinking, I'm not sure I really believe this. Part of me questioned the validity of "apart from me you can do nothing." After all, I had natural abilities, so what about those things? At last I began to understand. We can do things apart from the Lord that can entertain or look impressive to the world. However, if we hope to accomplish things that mean something in the Kingdom of God, apart from Christ we can do nothing.

Parable of the Sower: The Cultivated Heart

Jesus told a parable about a sower that went out to sow seed. Listen to what Jesus said as He explained this parable:

> [18] Listen then to what the parable of the sower means: [19] When anyone hears the message about the kingdom and does not understand it, the evil one comes and snatches away what was sown in their heart. This is the seed sown along the path. [20] The seed falling on rocky ground refers to someone who hears the word and at once receives it with joy. [21] But since they have no root, they last only a short time. When trouble or persecution comes because of the word, they quickly fall away. [22] The seed falling among the thorns refers to someone who hears the word, but the worries of this life and the deceitfulness of wealth choke the word, making it unfruitful. [23] But the seed falling on good soil refers to someone who hears the word and understands it. This is the one who produces a crop, yielding a hundred, sixty or thirty times what was sown. (Matt. 13:18-23)

In this parable, we see how our hearts are to become cultivated into the kind of hearts that are receptive to messages from the Kingdom of God.

Defeat Satan's Lies with God's Truth

Since Satan is the father of lies and specializes in deceit, we need to learn how to partner with the Holy Spirit of truth and say *no* to the lies from the enemy's camp. Satan wants to snatch away the Lord's calling from our hearts. When we hear the gospel message and seriously began to think about committing our lives to Jesus, the enemy will even seek to manipulate a friend by trying to influence them to talk us out of becoming a follower of Jesus. Satan would love to treat all of us like puppets on his string if we would allow him to.

Satan hates the ministry of the Holy Spirit and he will do everything he can to influence you in subtle ways to back away from knowing the Lord by partnering with the Holy Spirit through listening prayer. In today's world, we need the power and the leadership of the Holy Spirit every bit as much as the disciples did to be effective witnesses for Jesus. Jesus is the same yesterday, today, and forever. The Lord is capable of doing supernatural miracles today just as He has done in the past. God is willing to work through ordinary people of every generation if they will just say yes to whatever He wants to do in their lives. Why limit God in how he can use you? Let the Lord decide what your ministry will look like. But, you may say, this sounds different from what I was taught growing up. I encourage you to consider: Why not let the Lord have the place of ultimate authority for your life rather than religious tradition?

At Jesus' last supper with His disciples He took the cup and told them, "This cup is the new covenant in My blood, which is poured out for you" (Luke 22:20). Shortly after hearing this, the disciples began to argue about which of them was the greatest. I mean really, they really went there at a time like that! But notice the gospel writers were more interested in telling the truth about what happened rather than making themselves into idols to be adored. Listen to what Jesus said to Simon after the dispute: "[31] Simon, Simon, Satan has asked to sift all of you as wheat. [32] But I have prayed for you, Simon, that your faith may not fail. And when you have turned back, strengthen your brothers" (Luke 22:31-32).

When Satan is making a play to take down our callings from the Lord with his lies, we need to join in with the prayers that Jesus is praying for us from the throne room. We also need prayers from others on our behalf so that we will be strengthened and our faith will not fail. Praying through scripture is a powerful way to move into victory over Satan's deception. Paul lays out a great prayer strategy for us to pray over ourselves as well as for others when he tells us to put on our spiritual armor (Eph. 6:10-18). After we are equipped for battle with our spiritual armor firmly in place, Paul requests that his fellow soldiers would pray for him:

> [19] Pray also for me, that whenever I speak, words may be given me so that I will fearlessly make known the mystery of the gospel, [20] for which I am an ambassador in chains. Pray that I may declare it fearlessly, as I should. (Eph. 6:19-20)

Paul requested that others pray for him so that he could faithfully and powerfully proclaim the gospel. As someone who has preached a lot of sermons, I can tell you there is a world of difference preaching under the covering of prayer versus preaching without prayer support. Why not partner with the Holy Spirit of truth to confront the lies that are trying to steal the Lord's truths from our hearts! Satan does not want you to move into listening prayer because partnering with the Holy Spirit defeats him. We need to protect what the Lord is doing in our hearts by saying no to Satan's lies and yes to the Holy Spirit through listening prayer.

Sink Our Roots Deep in Christ

Back to the parable of the sower: we see people who were excited about the Lord and wanted to go deep with Him, yet they fell away when trouble or persecution came. Sometimes people will be excited initially about listening prayer, but when they are challenged or mocked by someone whose opinion they overvalue, they abandon ship and go back to their old worldly way of life. The enemy lies, telling them that they were just going through a God-phase and that what happened wasn't even real. If our desire is to have a receptive, cultivated heart, then we need to sink our roots deep in Christ and abide in Him. Then, when times of trouble or persecution come, we will stay strong in the Lord:

> [6] So then, just as you received Christ Jesus as Lord, continue to live your lives in him, [7] rooted and built up in him, strengthened in the faith as you were taught, and overflowing with thankfulness. [8] See to it that no one takes you captive through hollow and deceptive philosophy, which depends on human tradition and the elemental spiritual forces of this world rather than on Christ. (Col. 2:6-8)

Seek First the Kingdom of God

Finally in the parable of the sower, we come to the last obstacle to overcome so that our hearts will become like good soil that can bear an abundance of fruit. This challenge is about not letting the worries of this life and the deceitfulness of wealth choke out the word of the Lord in our hearts. Jesus told his disciples to seek first the Kingdom of God (Matt. 6:33). When we put God's plans and agenda first, we make the Lord the source of our security rather than worldly wealth. This moves us into living by faith into God's purposes and plans rather than living in fear. For many people, living in faith seems too scary. They crave security and don't want their Christian faith to make them feel uncomfortable. But why miss out on the incredible things that the Lord wants to do through our lives because of fear? When we come before the

Lord having decided that He is the source of our security, we open our hearts to hearing all that the Lord wants to say to us!

Our goal is for our hearts to be like the good soil that will bear a great crop out of the seed that was sown. When our hearts become like good soil, we fill our empty hearts with the Holy Spirit rather than with things from the world. So how about it, are you ready to remove brambles and pull up weeds from the garden of your heart to allow it to be fully engaged as you learn to listen to the Lord in prayer?

The Garden Hose and H_2O

Assuming you've said yes to the previous question, what does the process of allowing the Lord to cultivate your heart look like? Perhaps this illustration will help. When you go to listen to the Lord in prayer, you are like a garden hose. Your first job is to give yourself, the garden hose, to Jesus. Jesus takes you, the garden hose, and puts you on the spigot. God the Father turns the water on. The water is the Holy Spirit. It's the water that gives life, not the hose. Your job as the hose is quite simply to be a conduit to allow the water to get from point A to point B. But sometimes there are kinks in the hose and the water can't get through. The kinks in the hose are like the heart blockages that need to be removed. Once they are removed, you can receive what the Holy Spirit wants to communicate with you and through you.

Water, we learn in chemistry, is made up of two hydrogen atoms and one oxygen atom, expressed in the formula H_2O. I like to think this formula illustrates how to get the kinks out of the hose so that the Holy Spirit will flow through us to bring life to people. The first H stands for *hungry*, or being poor in spirit. We must have spiritual hunger to open the channel for God to work in and through us. The second H stands for *humble*. We must have humility—or in other words, get that pride out of the way— for God to work through us. The O stands for *obey*. We must be willing to act when God tells us to. Once we get the kinks out of the hose, we will have opened the way for the Holy Spirit to pour out life through us and into the people that we pray for.

After reading about the garden hose and H_2O, maybe you are saying, "Finally, something to do: let's make this happen!" Most of us have learned that the way to get good at something is through hard work and dedication. Wanting listening prayer in your life is important, to be sure, but there is a hidden issue here. If you have ever been a student, played sports, or performed music, you know what it is to compete and to try to be the very best at what you do. When you think about it, we are constantly in the mode of achieving as we go after the things that we care about. The countless hours of practice seem worth it when we finally achieve a goal that we have been going after.

One day I was preaching and found myself saying that partnering with the ministry of the Holy Spirit is not something we achieve, but something we receive. I love it when the Holy Spirit causes something to come out of my mouth that I have never thought before. Now this is a paradigm shift! It seems to be counterintuitive to the way that we live, though. Listen to what Jesus said right before He ascended so that we can move out of achieving and into receiving through listening prayer:

> Disciples: Is now the time, Lord—the time when You will reestablish Your kingdom in *our land of* Israel?
>
> Jesus: [7] The Father, on His own authority, has determined the ages and epochs *of history*, but you have not been given this knowledge. [8] *Here's the knowledge you need:* you will receive power when the Holy Spirit comes on you. And you will be My witnesses, first here in Jerusalem, then beyond to Judea and Samaria, and finally to the farthest places on earth. (Acts 1:8 VOICE)

One of the challenges of opening our hearts up to the Lord is the fear that we have of what the Lord may tell us. What if the Lord tells me to do something like move away from my home? This is exactly what the Lord told Abram to do:

> The LORD had said to Abram, "Go from your country, your people and your father's household to the land I will show you.
>
> 2 "I will make you into a great nation,
>   and I will bless you;
>   I will make your name great,
>   and you will be a blessing.
> 3 I will bless those who bless you,
>   and whoever curses you I will curse;
>   and all peoples on earth
>   will be blessed through you."
>
> 4 So Abram went, as the LORD had told him; and Lot went with him. Abram was seventy-five years old when he set out from Harran. (Gen. 12:1-4)

What if the Lord puts it on my heart to do a ministry that I don't think that I can perform? Moses felt that uncertainty when the Lord first talked to him through the burning bush:

> 11 But Moses said to God, "Who am I that I should go to Pharaoh and bring the Israelites out of Egypt?"
>
> 12 And God said, "I will be with you. And this will be the sign to you that it is I who have sent you: When you have brought the people out of Egypt, you will worship God on this mountain." (Exod. 3:11-12)

The key to Moses' ministry and ours is that God will be with us. Why let our fears thwart our destiny in the Lord for one more moment? Why not move into an incredible partnership with the Lord as your senior partner? In the following chapters, we will focus on learning to cooperate with the Holy Spirit as the Lord does some serious gardening in our hearts so that we can fulfill the very purpose for which we have been created. The Lord wants to cultivate our hearts so that we are open to receive His Kingdom assignments for our lives. I will never forget a prayer someone prayed for me: "The Lord is in the process of increasing your capacity to receive and is giving you a fire hose instead of a garden hose!" So, how about it, are you ready to increase your capacity to receive from the Lord?

Dear Lord, I confess that I have lived far below who I could have been for You and Your Kingdom. I repent for filling my heart with things from the world and not being filled with the Holy Spirit. I want to hear Your voice Lord, so I ask You to do in my heart whatever You have to do so that I will be able to follow the leading of the Holy Spirit for my life and ministry. In Jesus' name I pray. Amen.

CHAPTER 5

I Plead the Blood of Jesus

I plead the blood of Jesus and in the name of Jesus I command that only the Holy Spirit shall come close and prosper.

I've prayed this sentence thousands of times. I begin every listening prayer with it. At first, I prayed this way because it was how my mentor Brother Harold began his prayers. I have learned that making this declaration of faith honoring the cross of Jesus as a lead-in to listening prayer ushers us into the holiness of God's presence. I have witnessed over and over again how pleading the blood of Jesus activates partnering with the Holy Spirit in incredible ways. Pleading the blood of Jesus over prayer time is not the only way to hear from Jesus through listening prayer. But even if you are seasoned in partnering with the Holy Spirit's ministry through your prayers, I encourage you to ask the Lord if He wants you to honor the cross of Jesus in this way.

Some people are squeamish around blood. Even huge weight lifters have been known to pass out at the sight of blood. An aversion to blood makes the phrase "I plead the blood of Jesus" seem strange indeed. For some, it's a religious platitude best relegated to a bygone era. But there is so much power and holiness wrapped up in the phrase. *Plead* is a word from the courtroom.

Webster's 1828 Online Dictionary provides this definition:

> PLEAD, *verb intransitive* [...] In a general sense, to argue in support of a claim, or in defense against the claim of another.
>
> 1. In law, to present an answer to the declaration of a plaintiff; to deny the plaintiff's declaration and demand, or to allege facts which show that he ought not to recover in the suit. The plaintiff declares or alleges; the defendant pleads to his declaration. The king or the state prosecutes an offender, and the offender pleads not guilty, or confesses the charge.
>
> 2. To urge reasons for or against; to attempt to persuade one by argument or supplication; as, to *plead* for the life of a criminal; to *plead* in his favor; to *plead* with a judge or with a father.

When we plead the blood of Jesus over our time of prayer, we are coming before the holiness of God's presence in the righteousness of Jesus rather than in our own righteousness. Listen to the new relationship of right standing before God that has been made possible for us because of Jesus' death:

> [25] God presented Christ as a sacrifice of atonement, through the shedding of his blood—to be received by faith. He did this to demonstrate his righteousness, because in his forbearance he had left the sins committed beforehand unpunished— [26] he did it to demonstrate his righteousness at the present time, so as to be just and the one who justifies those who have faith in Jesus. (Rom. 3:25-26)

Notice the courtroom language used in the following scripture passage. This scripture passage describes what Jesus has done for us on the cross and the fact that we are declared not guilty when we put our trust and faith in Jesus. Also, notice the victory that the cross of Jesus made possible over the kingdom of darkness:

> 13 When you were dead in your sins and in the uncircumcision of your flesh, God made you alive with Christ. He forgave us all our sins, 14 having canceled the charge of our legal indebtedness, which stood against us and condemned us; he has taken it away, nailing it to the cross. 15 And having disarmed the powers and authorities, he made a public spectacle of them, triumphing over them by the cross.
>
> (Col. 2:13-15)

When we plead the blood of Jesus over our time of prayer, we are coming against the power of sin to pollute the process of us hearing from the Lord. Sin can dramatically impact the purity of what we receive in prayer. A word of caution is important here: the phrase "I plead the blood of Jesus" is not meant to come from a place of rote repetition. This phrase must come out of our relationship with the living God and through faith in God's beloved Son, Jesus. Scripture illustrates that using a formula in lieu of a relationship with Jesus is disastrous if we hope to move into the ministry of the Holy Spirit:

> 13 Some Jews who went around driving out evil spirits tried to invoke the name of the Lord Jesus over those who were demon-possessed. They would say, "In the name of the Jesus whom Paul preaches, I command you to come out." 14 Seven sons of Sceva, a Jewish chief priest, were doing this. 15 One day the evil spirit answered them, "Jesus I know, and Paul I know about, but who are you?" 16 Then the man who had the evil spirit jumped on them and overpowered them all. He gave them such a beating that they ran out of the house naked and bleeding. (Acts 19:13-16)

When we battle in the realm of the spirit, enemy spirits know who has a relationship with Jesus as Savior and Lord and who doesn't have that kind of a relationship. So, when we say "I plead the blood of Jesus" over our prayer time, we need to do so having truly repented of our sins and having truly yielded to Jesus' Lordship in our lives. Sometimes when people encounter a demonic manifestation for the first time, they are frightened because their lives are not right. When we plead the blood of Jesus, we need to do it with a heart desire to get our lives right with the Lord. We completely miss the point if we pray this phrase from the place of a disengaged heart or with unconfessed sin in our lives. Let's be honest, for those of us that have been part of the church for a long time, we have often treated holy things casually because our hearts were far from God.

One morning I had to get up early and travel to a nearby city to give a devotional at a prayer breakfast. A few minutes before the alarm went off, I woke up vividly remembering a dream. Up until that I point, I had never received a message from the Lord in a dream. I would tell people this: I don't dream; if I did dream I wouldn't remember it; and if I did remember a dream, I wouldn't know what it meant. When I first awoke, I realized quickly that not only did I remember the dream but that I knew what it meant. Fear quickly came upon me as I realized I was supposed to share the dream at the prayer breakfast.

On the way to the prayer breakfast, I picked up a student who told me that he and another student had been praying every night for two weeks that the Lord would speak to me in a dream. I thought, wow, that is amazing, and so I shared the dream with this student. Later, at the breakfast, I started my talk with a few humorous comments, then took a few deep breaths and dove in headfirst.

I said, "Christmas is coming up and every year we remember that God spoke to Joseph in a dream. Last night the Lord gave me a dream and I believe it is for us this morning. I dreamed I was leading a worship service where a bunch of kids were doing a baton twirling routine in the front of the church. I thought, who told them that they could do that? When they finished the routine, they decided to do the routine all over again. The service was finally turned over to me about ten minutes from its usual ending time. After racing through communion, I was completely out of time. The text I was getting ready to speak on was: 'The Spirit of the Lord is on me, because he has anointed me to proclaim good news' (Luke 4:18).

"As I looked out over the congregation, I saw a visiting pastor whom I knew would disapprove of what I was about to say. My message was that this passage of scripture showed that Jesus' supernatural ministry gave testimony to Him being the Son of God. As I looked at the people, I could tell that they wanted to leave even though I hadn't spoken yet. I decided to simply give the benediction and people left looking pretty happy. As I looked off to the side, I saw a bulletin that had an ink smudge on it. I thought, how did it get out of the office like this? I realized that the smudge was actually a group of words, 'Love us Lord.'

"This is what the dream means: we treat communion like a ritual that we have to hurry through. As long as we are entertained, it doesn't matter if we have heard from the Lord or not. The Lord is longing for our heart cry to be 'Love them, Lord, through us' instead of just 'Love us, Lord.'"

After my talk, I abruptly took a seat. After an awkward silence, a pastor stood up and prayed, "Thank you Lord for the message and the messenger," and gave a benediction. No one spoke to me, no one talked to each other, and everyone quietly left. The cross of Jesus is holy. Communion is holy. If we choose to use the sentence "I plead the blood of Jesus over this time of prayer and command that only the Holy Spirit shall come close and prosper," we need to do so with a fully engaged heart that honors the holiness of God. We need to pray this sentence from the place of us having a relationship with Jesus as our High Priest and King. Part of our ongoing relationship with Jesus means being honest and transparent about our lives with Jesus. Trying to hide our sin from Jesus is just not an option. Church history is scattered with notable leaders who were in sin, had not repented, and supposedly heard from the Lord when in fact they were being lied to by the enemy's camp. When we plead the blood of Jesus over our time of prayer, we are saying *no* to the ongoing interference of the power of sin. Using this phrase, however, presupposes that a deep repentance to the Lord has taken place:

> [5] This is the message we have heard from him and declare to you: God is light; in him there is no darkness at all. [6] If we claim to have fellowship with him and yet walk in the darkness, we lie and do not live out the truth. [7] But if we walk in the light, as he is in the light, we have fellowship with one another, and the blood of Jesus, his Son, purifies us from all sin.

> [8] If we claim to be without sin, we deceive ourselves and the truth is not in us. [9] If we confess our sins, he is faithful and just and will forgive us our sins and purify us from all unrighteousness. (1 John 1:5-9)

As we prepare to move into hearing from the Lord, repentance for past sins is crucial in preparing our hearts to meet with the Lord. Neal Anderson's book *Bondage Breaker* has an extremely effective repentance model that helps people get clean through the blood of Jesus. His repentance prayers for persons who have been involved in the occult are especially helpful.

When we plead the blood of Jesus over our time of prayer, we appropriate Jesus' victory over Satan's attempts to destroy our lives, and we enforce the victory that has been won in the realm of the spirit through the cross and resurrection of Jesus. Jesus called Satan a liar and the father of lies (John 8:44). When we plead the blood of Jesus, we come against Satan's power to lie to us in our time of prayer. Right after Simon Peter confessed that Jesus was the Christ, the Son of the living God, Peter rebuked Jesus when Jesus began to talk about the upcoming suffering he was going to endure on the cross:

> [31] Jesus then began to teach them that the Son of Man must suffer many things and be rejected by the elders, the chief priests and the teachers of the law, and that he must be killed and after three days rise again. [32] He spoke plainly about this, and Peter took him aside and began to rebuke him.
>
> [33] But when Jesus turned and looked at his disciples, he rebuked Peter. "Get behind me, Satan!" he said. "You do not have in mind the concerns of God, but merely human concerns." (Mark 8:31-33)

If Satan successfully lied to Peter right after Peter confessed that Jesus was the long-awaited Messiah, certainly it is possible that the enemy of our souls will try to slip his lies in on us. Peter warns us that even though the devil was ultimately defeated at the cross, we are still called to appropriate this victory by resisting him: "[8] Be alert and of sober mind. Your enemy the devil prowls around like a roaring lion looking for someone to devour. [9] Resist him, standing firm in the faith..." (1 Pet. 5:8-9).

In certain locations, spiritual interference can be tangible and aggressive. Those who pray on location for Jesus' name to go forward in power can testify how hard it can be sometimes to hear clearly from the Lord. Some years ago, I was in Louisville, Kentucky for a conference and had the opportunity to pray in the downtown area and around the University of Louisville for many to come to know Jesus as Savior and Lord. I was grateful I had learned to plead the blood of Jesus because the resistance was strong. Paul tells us that Satan blinds the minds of those who don't believe in Jesus: "The god of this age has blinded the minds of unbelievers, so that they cannot see the light of the gospel of the glory of Christ, who is the image of God" (2 Cor. 4:4).

Just a few months after I prayed in downtown Louisville, I learned that evangelist Billy Graham came to there to lead one of his last public preaching events to share the gospel with thousands of people. No wonder I had been led to pray for salvation in that place and no wonder there had been so much interference. It was also gratifying to realize that the Lord had probably alerted many other people to pray for this evangelistic outreach as well. As I talked about earlier, in Ephesians 6 Paul implores others to pray for him so that he could boldly proclaim the mystery of the gospel. Paul's request for prayer comes out of a spiritual warfare context in which he gives instructions about how to suit up for spiritual battle.

Jesus' cross and resurrection has assured us that the final outcome of the war has been won. However, the battle against Satan and his entourage is still raging on. Listen to these words of encouragement from the book of Revelation about appropriating the victory that is ours through the cross for this ongoing battle:

> [10] Then I heard a loud voice in heaven say:
>
> "Now have come the salvation and the power
> and the kingdom of our God,
> and the authority of his Messiah.
> For the accuser of our brothers and sisters,
> who accuses them before our God day and night,
> has been hurled down.
> [11] They triumphed over him
> by the blood of the Lamb
> and by the word of their testimony;
> they did not love their lives so much
> as to shrink from death.
> [12] Therefore rejoice, you heavens
> and you who dwell in them!
> But woe to the earth and the sea,
> because the devil has gone down to you!

He is filled with fury,
because he knows that his time is short."
(Rev. 12:10-12)

One of the enemy's favorite strategies is to attack people with lies to try to destroy their calling from the Lord. When the Spirit led Jesus into the wilderness, the enemy tried to steal Jesus' calling with lies. Jesus defeated every lie with truth from God's Word (Matt. 4:1-11). Since even Jesus was attacked in this way, we should not be surprised when the enemy tires to steal our callings from the Lord as well. Jesus was victorious over every scheme and plan of the enemy. The blood that Jesus shed on the cross enables us to walk in the victory that He won for us.

Presently I am sitting in a coffee house at a Christian university. The person I just prayed for has an incredible calling to love people that other people sometimes find difficult to love. Since this was her calling, the enemy was continually trying to lie to her that she wasn't loved. Satan loves to attack us at the place of our greatest calling. I found out after the prayer that she felt called to special education and that she really does feel called to love people that other people find it difficult to love.

When we do listening prayer, the Lord will often lead us to speak against the lies that the enemy sends to try to cripple people so that they won't step out in faith to walk into their destiny and calling. Pleading the blood of Jesus helps open the door to great victory through the cross of Jesus.

Also, when we plead the blood of Jesus in prayer, we resist the power of Satan's lies to disrupt the intimacy that the Lord longs to have with us. What Satan craves more than anything is our worship. When he tempted Jesus in the wilderness, Satan revealed that he was really after worship. Our hearts long for intimacy with God and Satan is jealous! Sadly, we often believe Satan's lies and try to satisfy the craving of our hearts from the world. But the good news is that Jesus through shedding His blood made intimacy with God possible. Because of His blood, we can "draw near to God with a sincere heart..." (Heb. 10:22).

Another way to think about the phrase "I plead the blood of Jesus" is to think of it as saying that we want to have communion with Jesus. Jesus gave his disciples a last supper to remember when they got together. At the Last Supper, we remember that our sins have been forgiven through Jesus: "[27] Then he took a cup, and when he had given thanks, he gave it to them, saying, "Drink from it, all of you. [28] This is my blood of the covenant, which is poured out for many for the forgiveness of sins" (Matt. 26:27-28).

This new testament or new covenant in Jesus' blood was so important in understanding what Jesus has done for us through His cross and resurrection that the New Testament in the Bible was named after what Jesus said here. Imagine the joy in heaven when we honor the cross of Jesus every time we go to listen to the Lord in prayer by praying "I plead the blood of Jesus" as way of expressing our longing to have communion with Jesus.

When we plead the blood of Jesus over our time of prayer, we are announcing to the realm of the spirit that we intend to have communion and fellowship with Jesus even in the presence of our enemies. Jesus, our Good Shepherd, is with us through every dark valley of life. When we plead the blood of Jesus, we are joining in the worship of heaven to Jesus, our Good Shepherd that shed his blood for us:

> [17] For the Lamb at the center of the throne
>   will be their shepherd;
>   "he will lead them to springs of living water."
>   "And God will wipe away every tear from their eyes."
>   (Rev. 7:17)

I could never have imagined that the phrase "I plead the blood of Jesus" would have become so important in my life. My hope is that you too will discover how pleading the blood of Jesus will bless your life and ministry for the Lord. Simon Peter learned through experience that the blood of Jesus was precious: "[18] ...it was not with perishable things such as silver or gold that you were redeemed from the empty way of life handed down to you from your ancestors, [19] but with the precious blood of Christ, a lamb without blemish or defect" (1 Pet. 1:18-19). Even though Peter denied Jesus and utterly abandoned Jesus during his time of greatest need, Peter became a champion of the Christian faith. Through his redeemed life, Peter shows us that we can become champions for Jesus as well. May this be said of us as it was said of Peter:

> [8] Then Peter, filled with the Holy Spirit, said to them: "Rulers and elders of the people! [9] If we are being called to account today for an act of kindness shown to a man who was lame and are being asked how he was healed, [10] then know this, you and all the people of Israel: It is by the name of Jesus Christ of Nazareth, whom you crucified but whom God raised from the dead, that this man stands before you healed. [11] Jesus is 'the stone you builders rejected, which has become the cornerstone.' [12] Salvation is found in no one else, for there is no other name under heaven given to mankind by which we must be saved."

> [13] When they saw the courage of Peter and John and realized that they were unschooled, ordinary men, they were astonished and they took note that these men had been with Jesus. (Acts 4:8-13)

Can you think of a better way to start listening in prayer than by honoring the cross of Jesus? One evening Grant prayed for me on the phone. He started with "I plead the blood of Jesus and I command that only the Holy Spirit shall come close and prosper." The peace that I immediately experienced after this was said was incredible. Although it spoke to my heart at the time, I have long forgotten what the rest of that prayer was about. But I will never forget the peace that rested upon me after the declaration about what the blood of Jesus continues to accomplish for us. Grant would be the first one to tell you that listening prayer is not about us: it's about Jesus.

In one of the early years of Pastor Daniel's ministry on campus, I was visiting him and his group. I slipped off to a side hallway to pray so that I could move deeper into the Lord's peace before I spoke that night. I was introducing listening prayer by praying for people in an effort to get spiritual hunger going. Sunyoung was a tenth grader at the time, but had become very hungry to hear from the Lord. So, listen, in Sunyoung's own words:

Open ears hear God speak peace

"The first time that I experienced listening prayer was when I was in 10th grade. We were getting ready for the praise night and I saw Pastor Tim sitting and praying in the hallway. I sat next to him and asked him to teach me to hear God. I still remember this very moment. Pastor Tim taught me to start my prayer by pleading the blood of Jesus Christ and taking captive every thought and only inviting the Holy Spirit to come close and prosper. Pastor Tim asked me to pray for him. I sincerely believed in those words and prayed and I waited. I heard His gentle voice and I heard the word 'peace'—how God wanted to use Pastor Tim for other people's lives with His great peace. It was a confirmation for both Pastor Tim and me. Pastor Tim was reaffirmed with God's calling on his life. God heard and saw my desperate yearning for Him and opened up my ears to hear Him."

The most noticeable characteristic of my mentor, Brother Harold, was the incredible peace that he walked in. Sunyoung's simple prayer for peace was a big deal to me because my heart had been for my life to radiate Jesus' peace the way that Brother Harold's life did.

I'd like to close this chapter with a benediction that I've used since I learned about pleading the blood of Jesus. May the truth of this powerful prayer of blessing and benediction from the book of Hebrews help us petition heaven with a new desire to have communion and fellowship with Jesus our Good Shepherd. May the Lord equip us from His heavenly storehouse so that we can do all our assignments as champions for the Lord Jesus Christ! Because of Jesus' great sacrifice, we can live life as sons and daughters of the King!

So, I pray it for you, and I hope you, too, will offer this scripture as prayer over your life and ministry:

> [20] *Now may the God of peace, who through the blood of the eternal covenant brought back from the dead our Lord Jesus, that great Shepherd of the sheep,* [21] *equip you with everything good for doing his will, and may he work in us what is pleasing to him, through Jesus Christ, to whom be glory for ever and ever. Amen.*
>
> *(Heb. 13:20-21)*

CHAPTER 6

Hunger to Hear the Voice of God

For ten hours I stood in line with thousands of people in the Florida sun. I was not at Disney World; I was in the parking lot of the Brownsville Assembly of God church in Pensacola, Florida. The guy behind me in line was from England. I asked him why he had come from so far to attend a worship service. He said that God was moving and he wanted to get in. Besides, he said, "I want to hear Jesus' voice." I said, "What is that?" He said, "You know, John 10:27." I asked again, "What are you talking about?"

In John 10:27, Jesus said, "My sheep listen to my voice, I know them, and they follow me." The Englishman said, "You know, the Holy Spirit wants to speak to us." Yet again, I asked, "What do you mean?" We talked a little further and I stood in line confused, intrigued, and curious. I thought to myself, whatever he is talking about, I'm interested! I had read the book of Acts, but like so many of the experiences described in it, the part about the Holy Spirit speaking was beyond my understanding. The supernatural experiences of the early disciples sounded like a foreign language that I didn't happen to speak. Even though I was a pastor, I had never heard anyone talk about hearing from the Holy Spirit and I felt I had never experienced anything like that myself. I once attended a charismatic house church in college and the atmosphere during worship there was the most alive feeling I had ever experienced, but other than that, the Holy Spirit was something that was just way beyond someone like me, or so I thought.

Seeing the Holy Spirit at work changing lives creates a hunger to partner with the Lord rather than going solo. Spiritual hunger is key to moving into the Lord's voice. Listen to what Jesus had to say about what we need to do to prepare to receive the ministry of the Holy Spirit in our lives:

> [9] "So I say to you: Ask and it will be given to you; seek and you will find; knock and the door will be opened to you. [10] For everyone who asks receives; the one who seeks finds; and to the one who knocks, the door will be opened.
>
> [11] "Which of you fathers, if your son asks for a fish, will give him a snake instead? [12] Or if he asks for an egg, will give him a scorpion? [13] If you then, though you are evil, know how to give good gifts to your children, how much more will your Father in heaven give the Holy Spirit to those who ask him!" (Luke 11:9-13)

At one of the revival services I attended at Brownsville, evangelist Steve Hill told a story about a service in which the Lord spoke to him in the middle of his message to stop and call someone out. Steve stopped and said, "There is a man here who cannot wait until the end of the message to respond to the altar call. You know the Lord is speaking to you so come down right now." A man ran to the front of the room and knelt at the altar. Later that evening, Steve asked what had happened and the man explained he had just prayed, "'God if you are real stop that guy in the middle of his message and call me out.' And then immediately you said what you did." This story lit a fire in my heart to know the Lord the way that Steve knew the Lord.

The Lord wants to fill us with and to lead us by the Holy Spirit if we will but ask. I don't know about you, but until my experiences at Brownsville, I had never asked. When I think about it now, the problem was that spiritual hunger was essentially missing from my life. Jesus promised that the Holy Spirit would be given to us in response to our asking, seeking, and knocking. This sure sounds like Jesus wants us to have spiritual hunger in our lives! The Holy Spirit was given to make His leadership available to us. In listening prayer, we ask for the leadership of the Holy Spirit. Being led by the Spirit is part of the inheritance that belongs to all believers in Christ. How the Holy Spirit leads may look different from person to person, but that the Holy Spirit is willing and able to lead us is a given:

> 14 For those who are led by the Spirit of God are the children of God. 15 The Spirit you received does not make you slaves, so that you live in fear again; rather, the Spirit you received brought about your adoption to sonship. And by him we cry, "Abba, Father." 16 The Spirit himself testifies with our spirit that we are God's children. 17 Now if we are children, then we are heirs— heirs of God and co-heirs with Christ, if indeed we share in his sufferings in order that we may also share in his glory. (Rom. 8:14-17)

When Paul talks about being a son or a daughter of God the Father because of our saving relationship with Jesus, He focuses on what is happening in the heart rather than on religious rituals that can only give the appearance of a right relationship with God. Before Paul met Jesus on the Damascus Road, Paul was all about religious rules and rituals. When Paul wrote this letter to the Romans, he had become a man of God who lived life by and in the Spirit.

Sometimes we have defined spiritual hunger as being present every time the church doors are open. Have you ever gone to church a whole lot and by all outward appearances had it all together, when in reality you were living a double life? Criticized that his disciples were not honoring the traditions of the elders because they not washing their hands before eating, Jesus replies that it is what comes out of the heart that really defiles a person:

> [16] "Are you still so dull?" Jesus asked them. [17] "Don't you see that whatever enters the mouth goes into the stomach and then out of the body? [18] But the things that come out of a person's mouth come from the heart, and these defile them. [19] For out of the heart come evil thoughts—murder, adultery, sexual immorality, theft, false testimony, slander. [20] These are what defile a person; but eating with unwashed hands does not defile them." (Matt. 15:16-20)

Once we recognize that we really aren't inherently "good people" and that it is in our best interest to repent of our sin, we open our hearts to receive the forgiveness that Jesus came to offer us through the cross. Through receiving Jesus, we are enabled to walk in hope. When sin gets entrenched in our lives, our spiritual hunger flies out the window. Thankfully the Holy Spirit is there to convict our hearts. Once we see clearly that we need the Lord's forgiveness, we have opened the door for spiritual hunger to increase in our lives. When we become poor in spirit, or desperate for God, and we begin to hunger and thirst for Jesus' righteousness, we begin to open the door to a love relationship with the Lord, and it's the only thing that can really fill us. After Jesus becomes our Lord and Savior, we can still allow sin in the back door and before we know it our passion for the Lord and our sense of purpose can come to a screeching halt.

I couldn't help but be drawn to the holiness of God's presence at Brownsville. The call for unbelievers and believers to give up sin and to follow Jesus felt so different there. The call to give up our sin was because you *wanted* to rather than because you *had* to. It truly was the holiness of God's presence that changed everything. There were lots of things going on that I did not understand, but the purity of the presence of God was unlike anything that I had ever known before. Jesus said that "blessed are the pure in heart for they will see God" (Matt. 5:8), and the atmosphere on those church grounds made a scripture verse like this suddenly make sense.

The Leadership of the Holy Spirit is Real

Months later a student and I took part in a time of intercessory prayer before one of the services at Brownsville. He told me as we walked away that he had received from the Holy Spirit that the evening was going to be about equipping leaders for ministry. That type of focus had never happened at any of the meetings I had been to. Later that evening, the speaker announced from the stage that the Holy Spirit had directed that the night was to be about equipping leaders for ministry, and while they never have that focus, they would follow the leadership of the Holy Spirit. At the announcement, I was in awe over the reality of the leadership of the Holy Spirit.

Experiences like this made me hungry to move into listening to God in prayer. The Lord was giving me a crash course in following the voice of the Holy Spirit. Maybe you have struggled, thinking that all of this hearing from the Lord stuff is fake Listen to what these students experienced that caused them to doubt their doubts!

A skeptic reacts

I will never forget this story about a couple of university students coming in to be prayed for with listening prayer by a member of our prayer team. What the person getting ready to pray for these students didn't know was that while they were standing out in the hallway, a skeptic in the group said that listening prayer wasn't real and that it was fake. "If this is real," she said, "the person praying will talk about these four specific things." When the intercessor began to pray, the skeptical student started freaking out. What she had just outlined out in the hallway was what the person prayed.

&

I share stories like this one to increase your hunger or to at least get you to consider the possibility that the Holy Spirit speaking today is real. Becoming poor in spirit and hungry for God is important in preparing to hear from the Lord in prayer. My hope is that you will begin to cry out to the Lord continually, "Lord I want to hear from you." That's what I did! Or what about this prayer: "I want to hear your voice Lord, please speak to me, and give me something hard to do, just speak to me." At first, all I heard was silence in response to these kinds of prayers, yet as time went on, my hunger to hear from the Lord became more and more intense.

You have your father's blessing

My dad, a pastor, died when my brother was a freshman in college. During college, my brother wondered if he should have gone into the ministry, too. Now, go forward in time about twenty years or so when my brother was attending a worship service that the pastor of the Brownsville church was leading in Auburndale, Florida. During prayer time at the church that night, the pastor walked over to a group of people where my brother was. He said, "The Lord is telling me that there is a man in this group whose father was a minister and whose brother is a minister. God has not called you into the ministry; let it go. Also, the Lord wants you to know that you have your father's blessing. You have your heavenly Father's blessing but the Lord also wants you to

know that you have your earthly father's blessing as well."
Needless to say, the prayer rocked my world because it was
so personal, and it was happening to my own brother, for
heaven's sake!

﷽

The Lord was giving me a crash course in how real the voice of the Holy Spirit is. Maybe, like the students standing out in the hallway, you have struggled with this hearing from the Lord stuff and feel it's all made up. But my hope in sharing listening prayer stories is that they will make you curious and hungry to hear from the Lord in prayer. God in His mercy wants us to know how much He loves us. When we receive personal words from the Lord in prayer that show us that God sees us and cares about us, we are overcome that with all the people in the world, the Lord cares about us as individuals. That God would want to communicate with individuals is beyond anything that we can comprehend. But that is how great the love of God is! My hope is that you will hear Jesus knocking on the door of your heart, and that you will be inspired to open the door of your heart and listen to Him.

Once you get hungry to hear the voice of the Lord in prayer, your motivation to learn goes through the roof. You will pray, "Teach me Lord, I am willing to learn and open to your instruction!" In an effort to learn more, I listened to recordings from Dr. Michael Brown of the Brownsville revival on listening to God. In this series, Dr. Brown shares a story that pushed me over the edge of wanting to hear from the Lord. He tells about an illiterate woman in India who went by the name Mother. When she went to a village, she would listen in prayer, the Lord would give her a scripture, someone else would read it, and then Mother would speak on it. One day she told a village the story of Jonah. No big deal— except she had never heard the story of Jonah before. The Lord told her the story of Jonah and then she told the people the story of Jonah. Dr. Brown sums up his reaction to the story of Mother: "I have a Ph.D. in Semitic languages, but I don't want my advanced learning to prevent me from knowing God the way this illiterate woman knows God."

So, move the clock ahead: the impossible had happened and the Lord had patiently brought me into listening prayer. I was praying by phone for a group of students gathered in an apartment in Atlanta, Georgia. I prayed for Nina, and the prayer got Nina's attention. She planned to call me later to ask about listening prayer. However, she decided that some big event needed to happen before she could call. One day she was in a car wreck so bad she could have been killed. She called and told me that this was a big enough event and that it was time to learn about listening prayer. She learned!

Not long after, at a listening prayer weekend, I was up at the front of the church speaking when my phone started vibrating. I looked down at my phone, and saw that it was Nina calling. I answered the phone right in the middle of my talk. I told Nina that I was with a group of friends and asked her to pray for them over speakerphone. She agreed. I put the speakerphone right next to the microphone and Nina proceeded to basically pray what I had just been sharing with the group. Later when I talked to Nina again, she asked if she had prayed for some folks over at my house and I said, "Oh no, I was speaking on listening prayer at the front of a church and I put my phone next to the microphone. Your prayer was awesome, thanks!" It's so much fun freaking college students out!

Keep Doing What You're Doing

On Tuesday nights, I meet with a group of young adults who go out in public and pray for people. After a time of worship and teaching, they go to the mall, grocery stores, and university campuses to pray for folks. After they finish praying,, we gather again and listen to the stories about how Jesus touched people. Honestly, hearing each other's stories makes you really hungry to be used by the Lord through listening prayer. One young adult, her face radiant with light, shared that praying for others had been the most exciting experience of her life. Her enthusiasm was so inspiring! It is amazing when we overcome our fears and reach out to touch others with the love of Jesus through prayer. Sometimes the *no*'s we get will even make us hungry for more. Chance and Zach went out and were getting ready to ask a guy if they could pray for him in a grocery store. He interrupted them before they could even ask by saying "No, I'm not interested." As they walked away, they told him that Jesus loved him and he told them that Jesus loved them, too. Chance told us that normally a person saying *no* doesn't get to him but that this particular *no* did! Afterwards, he said that he went over to the yogurt section to sulk for about ten minutes. We all busted out laughing because we knew exactly how he felt! A dad who was with us that night told us that people often approached him like this before he was a Christian and that he had responded very negatively until one day he received Christ in his life. He encouraged us to keep doing what we were doing. (You *know* you want to try this!)

Jeremy was in my youth group when he was in 10th grade and then I became his youth pastor for a short four-month stint when he was the lead pastor of a church in Arizona. I don't know if you think that is funny, but I do. Nelson told me, "You do realize that you are too old to do something like this." I told him, "Evidently not." Nelson went on to say, "I guess you think that the Lord is telling you to do this." I told him, "Evidently so."

I digress, so, on to a listening prayer story from Pastor Jeremy.

Jesus loves the little children

"We had traveled to Nicaragua for a mission trip... No specific agenda, just to follow wherever the Lord leads. Our team all had the ability to hear from the Lord, so we agreed going in that if the Lord led us in different directions that

would be OK. We had spent most of the trip together and had done some really cool ministry. We had prayer walked around the atheist president's home. We had ministered at a school. We ministered at a local church through leading worship and preaching. Finally we had all gathered together to go and minister to the impoverished people living in the city dumps. We spent the whole day delivering food, clothing, toys, and sharing the Gospel with hundreds of people in the dump. When we had finished our work that day, we were all completely worn out and irritable. Part of the group wanted to spend the next day doing tourist activities. As we prayed through it, some of us heard the Lord say, 'You're not done at the dump yet.' That news didn't sit well with the whole team. They had worked very hard and deserved some rest from their labor. After some heated discussion, we finally remembered our covenant with one another—if we felt called to do different things, that was OK. So, two of us made arrangements to go back to the dump while the rest of our team headed off for a day of fun and relaxation.

"While at the dump that day, we met a very young mother who had a very sick baby. The baby was born with Down syndrome, and was also very malnourished. The poor child had been suffering from diarrhea for over two weeks. She was very close to death's door, and without intervention she would be meeting Jesus very quickly. When we met this child, and held her in our arms, we knew that she was the reason why the Lord had told us to go back. Her family had absolutely nothing. They lived in a tin hut, with a roof made from used garbage bags. The floor was nothing but dirt, and it was covered in trash from their daily foraging for food. Her father had just been badly injured while working on their home, and was unable to work. This precious baby girl was in dire straits.

"After praying over the child, we took her to the local pharmacy and purchased the medicine that she would need to recover from her diarrhea. We purchased electrolyte-enhanced drinks to help her rehydrate, and finally we purchased her a month's worth of formula to help her regain her strength and nutrition. Who knows what God has in store for this baby girl! But that day, God rescued that little girl. Listening to the Lord and following His instruction can have life changing and lifesaving results!"

When I am first introducing people to listening prayer, I find it important to pray for them and to share testimonies about how real the love of God is through listening prayer. I have intentionally shared listening prayer stories throughout this book from a wide variety of voices. We have a tendency in the church to see some people as rock stars and to see that what they are doing as inaccessible to us common folks. I have so appreciated Todd White. Todd White is one of the boldest witnesses for Jesus I have ever known in my life. The stories that he shares about ministering to people in public have challenged me to do things for the Lord that previously would not have happened. Todd's *YouTube* videos have inspired a whole generation to step into their identity as sons and daughters of Jesus our King. Todd is helping the body of Christ learn a new normal! My identity was so wrapped up in being afraid of what people thought and in people-pleasing that I was living far below the Lord's design for my life. So, a shout out of thanks to Todd! I will never forget driving alongside a parkway in Kentucky for miles because I could not find an on ramp. At one point, I drove over the parkway and then later I drove under the parkway—still no on-ramp. Finally, I found one. My hope is that this book will help show you where the on-ramp is to listening to the Lord in prayer! What if you laid down the unbelief that you have had toward yourself? What if you came to the conclusion that the Lord delights in sharing His voice with ordinary people? What if the Lord really wants us to know Him as the early disciples knew Him in the book of Acts?

There is no way to describe the joy I have in taking a team of young adults to a university campus and then praying for students on the sidewalk. Last year José, Kelsey, and I got to go to a campus where we prayed for quite a few people. Kelsey had graduated from the college that we went to and evidently what happened when we prayed for people was quite the talk on campus. José shared this story with me about what happened when Kelsey got to pray for Meagan with listening prayer:

A calling confirmed

"Meagan was a new believer wondering what was available for her in the Lord. With many doubts and questions, she was affirming her confidence and destiny with the Lord. The day that Kelsey prayed for her, she really needed some encouragement. She was about to go on a school field trip to Costa Rica and was afraid that it was going to weaken her faith. Kelsey prayed without knowing her: 'Thank you Lord that you are going to send Meagan to the nations, especially South America, and that she will be leading many to worship the Lord.' When she said this, Meagan had no clue that her Costa Rica trip was going to turn into a mission trip, and that she was going to be leading many Costa Ricans to worship Jesus a month later! She got invited to lead worship (for the first time) at a church, and that day the Lord confirmed that she was called to be a missionary and worshiper of the Lord. Praise God that He speaks to build our confidence as sons and daughters."

Here is what I have discovered in helping people move into experiencing listening prayer: spiritual hunger has to be present or people will drift away. If spiritual hunger is not there, listening to the Lord in prayer becomes just another temporary obsession to discard when the next fad comes along. We have to be willing for the Lord to put the fire of His presence in our hearts and we need to determine that to the best of our ability we fully intend to follow Jesus by obeying His voice. So how about you, are you ready to go after following Jesus with all of your heart by listening in prayer?

Dear Lord, please teach me how to hear Your voice. Please increase my hunger, Lord, to know You in this way. Please put a fire in my heart, Lord, of Your power and presence and leadership that will never go out. In Jesus' name, I pray. Amen.

CHAPTER 7

The Secret Blessing of Loneliness

oneliness can be incredibly painful. I once heard a student describe the atmosphere on a university campus in the fall when school is just starting: "It's like there is something really exciting going on, but somehow you're not a part of it." On the other end of the age spectrum, loneliness is embodied by the person who has just lost their spouse after 60 years of marriage. Since loneliness seems to be part of the human condition, how do you deal with it? For many who struggle with addiction, that addiction is often driven by the desire to escape loneliness. But loneliness is not always a bad thing. In learning to listen to God, loneliness can be the very thing to fuel the fire of passion in your life to draw close Jesus. When the Holy Comforter shows up in that lonely place, it's life changing.

Some of us were praying for college students one night at a prayer gathering at a house in Indiana. A prayer for Emily (name changed) stood out because it was so unique: "It's like you are really lonely. You are in this castle and no one can get to you. There is this moat around the castle and the draw bridges have been drawn up and no one can get to you." Toward the end of the prayer, the person who was praying received to thank God that Jesus was Emily's prince. Emily started crying. Later that evening I heard this story about Emily. She said, "I was just talking to my friend and telling her how lonely I have been feeling. My friend said to me, 'I have been feeling really lonely too. It's like I'm in this castle and no one can get to me. There is a moat around the castle and the drawbridges have been drawn up.' I said, 'I feel the same way.' After the conversation, I went to the library and checked out a book with the story about Rapunzel (the girl with the long hair trapped in a castle). When I read the part about the prince coming to save her, I started crying." Jesus loves us so much, He really does. He longs to meet with us in the lonely places. He doesn't want us to hide our feelings. Heartache and pain from loneliness when rightly seen is like a fire to draw us close to the heart of Jesus.

C.S. Lewis, an atheist who began to doubt his atheism, speaks to the heart-longing that he began to take seriously: "If we find ourselves with a desire that nothing in this world can satisfy, the most probable explanation is that we were made for another world." After considerable struggle, he came to faith in Jesus. Experiencing listening prayer helps us to know that our true home is not this world; our true home is with Jesus. At a youth retreat with Pastor Paul, I prayed for a 10th grader, "The Lord says welcome home." A little later I prayed, "The Lord is healing your broken heart." I got the most incredible note from this student about what the prayers meant to her. The comfort the Holy Spirit gives us in the lonely places is hard to describe, but very, very real.

One of the things that we unintentionally do is to put our best foot forward at church and hide disappointment, loneliness, and pain in our lives. When you are sitting or standing in physical or psychological pain, it is hard to engage with what is going on. Yet, we often put on a smile to cover our true feelings, and then, unfortunately, simply going through the motions is just around the corner. Eventually, we can begin to suspect that the Christian faith will never connect with the deepest parts of who we are.

Somehow, we think that the empty, surface-only comments we give and receive is just the way it is, and we lower our expectation levels. The temptation when the pain of loneliness hits our hearts is to turn to something, anything to make the pain go away. It never occurs to us that the pain could be fuel for the fire that could draw us close to the heart of the Lord. Let's face it, many things distract us from pursuing a personal relationship with the Lord. When the pain of loneliness hits hard, other things vie for our attention and the Lord just doesn't seem to be a significant player in our lives at this place of pain.

Loneliness can easily pull us away from the Lord if we turn to the world to fill the void we feel. We start out seriously pursuing the Lord, but as we yield to worldliness, before we know it, we have moved into apathy and boredom. We are prone to losing our spiritual hunger for the Lord. As I've said before, repentance needs to be a regular part of our lives. We need to ask the Lord to help us fall out of love with the world and in love with Him. Listen to what Jesus said about how falling in love with the world can blind us to who He wants to be in our lives:

> [16] For God so loved the world that he gave his one and only Son, that whoever believes in him shall not perish but have eternal life. [17] For God did not send his Son into the world to condemn the world, but to save the world through him. [18] Whoever believes in him is not condemned, but whoever does not believe stands condemned already because they have not believed in the name of God's one and only Son. [19] This is the verdict: Light has come into the world, but people loved darkness instead of light because their deeds were evil. [20] Everyone who does evil hates the light, and will not come into the light for fear that their deeds will be exposed. [21] But whoever lives by the truth comes into the light, so that it may be seen plainly that

what they have done has been done in the sight of God. (John 3:16-21)

Repentance helps us to break up with the world and open the door to intimacy with Jesus. Falling in love with the world kills spiritual hunger. If you are really hungry for food, but eat cotton candy instead, it may taste good going down, but eventually it makes you sick to your stomach. Our hearts are hungry for the things of God, but instead of running to the Lord, we fill up on things that make our souls sick. We run to things that supposedly will give us fulfillment or a sense of intimacy and the next thing we know, we have no hunger for God. Instead of loneliness being the catalyst to cause us to run hard after the Lord, it has the potential to cause us to run hard after the things of the world.

False Loneliness Solution: Pathway to Addiction

Satan's favorite solutions to the loneliness hitting our hearts are pornography, drugs and alcohol, obsessing over our appearance, and serial relationships. These high-voltage activities and relationships promise excitement and fulfillment but deliver emptiness and a sin-sick soul instead. The Lord wants to put His pictures and words deep into our hearts so that we will know how holy and loving He is. Satan knows this, so he appeals to our lusts and craving for excitement to rob us of the intimacy with the Lord that our hearts long for. He knows that if he can give us a false substitute, he can hide from us the tremendous destiny and calling that the Lord has for our lives. So, if you will, Satan does everything he can to fill up our hard drives (hearts) with his nonsense so that he can block us from hearing the voice of the Lord in prayer. He knows that if he can get us into addictive activities and relationships, he can easily distract us from discovering the exciting adventures that the Lord wants to take us on. Satan hates the Holy Spirit, so he knows if he can harden our hearts with the constant pursuit of worldly cravings, then we won't sign up to be radically Holy Spirit led people that shine the light of Christ into the darkness.

Since the craving for more has been used so strategically by the enemy's camp to take advantage of a person's loneliness and to steal intimacy with Jesus, I thought I'd share a few things that will help us use loneliness to strengthen our relationship with the Lord rather than to weaken it. Just making a passing reference to these painful addictions and problems with no help offered typically makes people feel more shame, guilt, and anger. When this happens, the destructive cycle of loneliness, craving what is destroying us, and becoming further alienated from God continues to spiral downward. Jesus wants to set us free of this so that we can move into intimacy with Him.

> [1]Therefore, rid yourselves of all malice and all deceit, hypocrisy, envy, and slander of every kind. [2]Like new-born babies, crave pure spiritual milk, so that by it you may grow up in your salvation, [3]now that you have tasted that the Lord is good. (1 Pet. 1:1-3)

Loneliness Cure: CRAVE the Lord

I use the acrostic CRAVE to help turn loneliness into an asset instead of a liability. What if we were to ask the Lord to transform our craving for the world into a new kind of craving?

> **C**ry out to Jesus
> **R**esist the devil and he will flee from you
> **A**uthenticity with others
> **V**ictory at the foot of the cross
> **E**xperience God

C The first phrase of CRAVE is "Cry out to Jesus." Blind Bartimaeus cried out to Jesus because he saw in Jesus the one person that could help him:

> [47] "Jesus, Son of David, have mercy on me!"
>
> [48] Many rebuked him and told him to be quiet, but he shouted all the more, "Son of David, have mercy on me!"
>
> [49] Jesus stopped and said, "Call him."
>
> So they called to the blind man, "Cheer up! On your feet! He's calling you." [50] Throwing his cloak aside, he jumped to his feet and came to Jesus.
>
> [51] "What do you want me to do for you?" Jesus asked him.
>
> The blind man said, "Rabbi, I want to see."
>
> [52] "Go," said Jesus, "your faith has healed you." Immediately he received his sight and followed Jesus along the road. (Mark 10:46-52)

Bartimaeus started screaming at the top of his lungs in spite of all the people around him who told him to shut up. Bartimaeus was not to be deterred. I once saw Steve Hill bang a metal cup and plate together and cry out to Jesus at the top of his lungs from a platform at Brownsville. This cry shook me to the core of my being. The first step of freedom from our worldly cravings is to know that Jesus is the One to whom we need to cry out. If you need to, be like Charles Finney, the famous evangelist in the Second Great Awakening in the United States, and cry out to Jesus at the top of your lungs out in the woods somewhere! This is no time to give Jesus a polite golf clap; give him all you've got. I followed Steve's example one time and banged a metal plate and a cup together in my sermon and cried out to Jesus at the top of my lungs in front of a group of college students. It shook all of us up, including me. I mean, really! Cry out to Jesus!

R The next phrase in CRAVE is "Resist the devil and he will flee from you." Listen to what James has to say about this: "⁷ Submit yourselves, then, to God. Resist the devil, and he will flee from you. ⁸ Come near to God and he will come near to you. Wash your hands, you sinners, and purify your hearts, you double-minded" (James 4:7-8).

Jesus modeled for us that using the Word of God is an incredibly powerful way to resist the devil when we are being tempted (Matt. 4:1-11). This scripture passage is an amazing way to wrestle lust down to the ground:

> ³ For though we live in the world, we do not wage war as the world does. ⁴ The weapons we fight with are not the weapons of the world. On the contrary, they have divine power to demolish strongholds. ⁵ We demolish arguments and every pretension that sets itself up against the knowledge of God, and we take captive every thought to make it obedient to Christ. (2 Corinthians 10:3-5)

Memorize this scripture, or put it on your phone and use it as your battle cry when temptation or the devil's lies try to take you down. Some of the enemy's favorite lies include "What you are doing isn't hurting anyone" and "Everybody is doing it." He also loves this lie: "You really don't have a problem, and you can stop any time that you want." Treat these lonely thrills for what they are, a flagrant attack against your identity, your destiny, your calling, and an attempt to substitute fake intimacy for intimacy with the Father, Son, and Holy Spirit. So how about it, why not use the Word of God as your sword and throw down!

A The next phrase in CRAVE is "Authenticity with others." Scripture tells us that Satan prowls around like a roaring lion, seeking whom he may devour. Out in the wild, one of a lion's favorite strategies is to isolate one of the animals from the herd. Cravings become very difficult to resist when someone is isolated with no one to pray for them. Listen to what James had to say: "¹⁶ Therefore confess your sins to each other and pray for each other so that you may be healed. The prayer of a righteous person is powerful and effective" (James 5:16). Finding godly people to stand with you and pray for you is essential to moving into the relationship with Jesus that you were born to have!

V The next phrase in CRAVE is "Victory at the foot of the cross." "Overwhelming victory is ours through Christ who loved us enough to die for us" (Rom. 8:37 TLB). When we humble ourselves at the foot of the cross and plead the blood of Jesus over our lives, we open the door to great victory! It's a great idea to go on offense and to plead the blood of Jesus over your room, your computer, your phone, and over the close relationships in your lives. Why not take ground back that the enemy has stolen from your life?

E CRAVE's last phrase is "Experience God." Late night belongs to the Lord. What Satan craves is worship. What better way to resist temptation than to reserve late nights to worship the Lord? When you are by yourself and it's late at night, how about ending the evening by putting some worship music on with headphones and reading a Bible on your phone instead of looking at videos or pictures or feeding addictions; why not draw close to Jesus through listening prayer instead? Why don't we join in with Paul's prayer from the book of Ephesians and ask that this prayer would become a reality in our lives and in the lives of the group that we are being authentic with?

> ¹⁷... I pray that you, being rooted and established in love, ¹⁸ may have power... to grasp how wide and long and high and deep is the love of Christ, ¹⁹ and to know this love that surpasses knowledge—that you may be filled to the measure of all the fullness of God. (Eph. 3:17-19)

James has intense things to say about what worldliness does to our prayers:

> [1] What causes fights and quarrels among you? Don't they come from your desires that battle within you? [2] You desire but do not have, so you kill. You covet but you cannot get what you want, so you quarrel and fight. You do not have because you do not ask God. [3] When you ask, you do not receive, because you ask with wrong motives, that you may spend what you get on your pleasures. [4] You adulterous people, don't you know that friendship with the world means enmity against God? Therefore, anyone who chooses to be a friend of the world becomes an enemy of God. (James 4:1-4)

There is something incredibly freeing when we admit that we have become attached to the wrong things. Hey, let's call this what it is: it's idolatry:

> Since, then, you have been raised with Christ, set your hearts on things above, where Christ is, seated at the right hand of God. [2] Set your minds on things above, not on earthly things. [3] For you died, and your life is now hidden with Christ in God. [4] When Christ, who is your life, appears, then you also will appear with him in glory. [5] Put to death, therefore, whatever belongs to your earthly nature: sexual immorality, impurity, lust, evil desires and greed, which is idolatry. (Col. 3:1-5)

Why play the game of prideful pretending one second longer? Why not turn away from worldly things that try to steal our relationship with the God who made us?

What Satan wants is your worship. If the enemy can get you to worship God's creation instead of the creator, he has started us down the pathway to getting the worship he is craving. So instead of worshipping porn or relationships, why not worship the Lord instead? Worshipping at the feet of Jesus is what your heart is longing for even if you don't know it at this moment in time. What I'm saying may sound ridiculous to you. But once you experience the presence of the Lord, you will never be the same. Once you experience the love relationship with the Lord that you were designed for, you will do everything you can to protect that relationship, because it is the one thing that replaces loneliness. (Yeah, right. No, *really*, why not pursue Jesus? A personal relationship with Jesus is what you've always wanted even if you don't know this at this point in time!)

I paraphrase here what Steve Hill from the Brownsville revival used to say: "When the party is over and you are by yourself and it is late at night, you know that something is terribly wrong, and the something that is wrong is in here (Steve would point to his heart at this point)." Loneliness and disappointment, as painful as they are, have the potential to be transformed into spiritual hunger to hear the voice of the Lord if we turn to the Lord rather than to things in the world to satisfy our hearts. What our hearts long for is intimacy, and hearing the voice of the Lord is a form of intimacy that we never know how badly we need until we actually experience it in our lives.

The Holy Spirit wants to change us into world-changing, adventure-seeking followers of Jesus who are sold out for the Kingdom of God. The Holy Spirit wants to connect us with Jesus and God the Father. The Holy Comforter wants to help us hear the voice of Jesus, our Good Shepherd. For those of us who pray with listening prayer for others, we continually see people surprised by the incredible love of Jesus. One of the common reactions people have to listening prayer is "Where has this been all my life?"

One evening I had the privilege of introducing a group of college students to listening prayer through a Bible study. I brought along a team of young adults that had moved into listening prayer. After the study, we began praying for the students. One came over to me and said, "We've got to talk!

Seven different people came over to me at different times and they all prayed the same thing for me. I don't know what this is, but I have to have this in my life." That's exactly the way I felt when someone first prayed for me with listening prayer: I have to have this in my life!

The news about Jesus' healing ministry traveled like wildfire everywhere he went. Jesus exploded onto the scene and everyone tried to get close to Him. In these verses, we see His secret power source to fulfilling His mandate from heaven to seek and to save the lost: "[15] Yet the news about him spread all the more, so that crowds of people came to hear him and to be healed of their sicknesses. [16] But Jesus often withdrew to lonely places and prayed" (Luke 5:15-17).

Jesus, our Good Shepherd, is inviting us to run to Him and pray especially when we are covered over with waves of loneliness. I will never forget being on an island at a youth retreat and leaving the cabin in the middle of the night to sit on the beach and listen to the waves crashing in. At that time, I was searching for a deeper relationship with the Lord but I just didn't know how to get there. When loneliness hits us and we run to the lonely place to meet with Jesus, we open the door to hearing His voice in extraordinary ways. Less than two hours after I typed this story into this chapter, I had the opportunity to pray for John. After praying for him, he prayed for me with listening prayer. During the prayer he said, "Pastor Tim, I see you sitting by the edge of the ocean and you are watching the waves coming in and the Lord's peace is coming upon you." Later in the prayer John thanked the Lord that when I am alone, I get to be with the Lord. What a joy it was to share the story I had just written about sitting by the ocean watching the waves coming in with John and to tell him how I was writing about how loneliness can lead us closer to the Lord.

He Sees You and Knows You

One evening, some of the members of our prayer team were praying for people at a local church. One of the people that we prayed for that night had been praying that day, "Lord, do you even see who I am?" This is such a big world with so many people in it. If you have ever been to a large city with lots and lots of people you can really appreciate this. Sometimes one of the loneliest places to be is walking by yourself in a downtown area with huge crowds of people. So, this awesome person decided to let some of our team pray for her. One of the first things that happened in the prayer was that one of the persons thanked the Lord that He saw who she was. This person blew it off and thought that this was just a coincidence. After the prayer, the person that had just prayed suggested that another member of the team pray for her. This prayer started the same way, "The Lord wants you to know that He sees who you are." Again, the person being prayed for blew it off thinking that this was yet another coincidence. The previous person that had prayed came over and said emphatically, "The Lord wants you to know that beyond a shadow of doubt, HE... SEES... WHO... YOU... ARE!" When these words were spoken in prayer, the person being prayed for burst into tears and said months later that this encounter with the Lord literally changed her life.

The Lord in His great love for us wants to come into the lonely places of our lives and set us free to become all that we could become for Him. So instead of seeing loneliness as this painful thing that we want to avoid at all costs, why not see loneliness as fueling a fire in our hearts to really know the Lord and His will and plan for our lives. For a very intense period of King David's life, he was running for his life from King Saul. He spent a great deal of time in caves and in rocky desolate places. When King David went through lonely times, it would often lead him to cry out to the Lord:

¹⁴ The LORD confides in those who fear him;
    he makes his covenant known to them.
¹⁵ My eyes are ever on the LORD,
    for only he will release my feet from the snare.
¹⁶ Turn to me and be gracious to me,
    for I am lonely and afflicted.
¹⁷ Relieve the troubles of my heart
    and free me from my anguish. (Psalm 25:14-17)

What if our loneliness could actually be what we need so that we would cry out to the Lord to confide in us the way that King David did?

Take His Hand

Leslie Weatherhead shares a story in his book, *The Transforming Friendship*. He tells about a man who was close to death in an incredibly lonely place in his life. His pastor came to see him and explained how Jesus wanted to have fellowship with him. The pastor pulled a chair over to his bed and encouraged the man to reach out and take Jesus by the hand. Jesus promised us "I am with you always" at the end of the Great Commission. Even though we might not be able to see Him or feel the touch of his hand, He is still there. Later on, the housekeeper told the pastor that when the man died, he had his hand on the chair next to his bed. I read this story in my twenties, and it captivated my heart. How could I have ever imagined how the Lord was using this story to set me up for encounters with Him? Listening prayer helps us take Jesus, our Good Shepherd, by the hand.

One of my favorite childhood memories was going to a Pittsburg Pirates spring training game with the New York Yankees. I got to see Roberto Clemente, Mickey Mantle, Roger Maris, and Bobby Richardson play. The memory that stands out to me, though, is a of a man who was drunk that grabbed on to me. I felt no fear whatsoever because my dad had me by the hand. For these reasons, one of the most powerful images of faith for me has been taking Jesus by the hand. At a critical moment in time that was demanding a great deal of faith, a student prayed for me and said, "Pastor Tim, I don't know what this means to you but I saw a construction worker holding a little kid by the hand and I feel like the Lord wants you to know that He has you by the hand." The Holy Spirit helps us to walk in faith—how wonderful is that?

At the last minute, the Lord's provision came in and I memorized this verse as a standing stone (Josh. 4) to remember what the Lord had done:

> So do not fear, for I am with you;
> do not be dismayed, for I am your God.
> I will strengthen you and help you;
> I will uphold you with my righteous right hand.
> (Isa. 41:10)

Jesus' love made real

Years later a team of us got to pray for some students from Lexington that had come over to our prayer time in Louisville, Kentucky. This prayer team had made the commitment to learn how to hear from the Lord even though doing so was foreign to them at first. We prayed for Jenna with listening prayer. She was deeply touched by the love of Jesus during the prayer time. Marvin, John, Lisa, Jean, and I all prayed for her and she was blown away! She had been struggling with school because she felt distracted and depressed because of what she had gone through. She cried all the way home to Lexington because the love of Jesus was now so real! Jenna said that she felt like this was when she was baptized in the Holy Spirit. Jenna was no longer the same person at school. In fact, she went on to complete her Ph.D. in nursing. This verse became meaningful for Jenna: "For now we see only a reflection as in a mirror; then we shall see face to face. Now I know in part; then I shall know fully, even as I am fully known" (1 Cor. 13:12).

Jenna said that before the prayer time, she didn't realize how much Jesus really loved her. The prayers helped her to understand how deep his love was. Jenna said that when she sees Jesus in heaven someday, she will get to fully know His love, but the prayers helped her to know that she was currently known by Him.

Jenna came back to see us in Louisville and she was beginning to learn how to listen in prayer. I got in prayer to tell her that she needed to be willing to pray for pastors. She said, "Ok, I get it, I get it; I think that I'm supposed to pray for you. I was hearing that but doubted it." She started by saying, "This probably doesn't mean anything to you but I am getting this verse for you: "So do not fear, for I am with you; do not be dismayed, for I am your God. I will strengthen you and help you; I will uphold you with my righteous right hand" (Isa. 41:10).

I told Jenna that the first time I had faced unemployment I had memorized this verse when I was able to get a job at the last minute, and it was a rock for me during that uncertain time. Now that I was facing the possibility of unemployment again, I told her that the Holy Spirit had highlighted that verse because He knew how much that was going to mean to me.

His Voice Leads

I have experienced up close and personal how Jesus, our Good Shepherd, takes us by the hand when we walk through dark valleys. He holds us, and guides us. He speaks, if only we will listen.

²⁷ My sheep listen to my voice; I know them, and they follow me. ²⁸ I give them eternal life, and they shall never perish; no one will snatch them out of my hand. (John 10:27-28)

Why not let loneliness cause you to take Jesus by the hand and listen to his voice? Praying scripture is an incredible way to take Jesus by the hand! Psalm 23 is another of King David's powerful prayers that is especially powerful in helping people transform loneliness to help them walk closer with Jesus our Good Shepherd. Praying Psalm 23 is an amazing way to affirm our relationship to Jesus as our Good Shepherd and to open our hearts to His Voice. Why not try a faith experiment: why not pray Psalm 23 and reach out to take Jesus by the hand even though you may not see Him with your eyes. Who knows, maybe the Lord in His mercy will allow you to see Jesus there with you! But even if we don't see Him with our physical eyes or with a picture on the inside, we still receive His presence in our lives through faith. So how about it, why not pause and pray through Psalm 23 (KJV).

¹ The Lord is my shepherd; I shall not want.

Jesus, thank You for being my Good Shepherd. What my heart really needs is a relationship with You. I am sorry for all the times I have blown You off and for how I have sought to fill my heart with the world instead of with a relationship with You. Jesus, hearing Your voice is what I really need.

² He maketh me to lie down in green pastures: he leadeth me beside the still waters.

Jesus, thank You that in your presence is the one place I can safely lay down all of my fears. Jesus, I ask for Your peace to overcome all of my fears. Jesus, it's my desire to learn to follow the leading of the Holy Spirit. Teach me how to walk with You, Jesus, by listening to Your voice.

³ He restoreth my soul: he leadeth me in the paths of righteousness for his name's sake.

Thank You, Jesus, that You restore my soul when loneliness and disappointment seem to want to come in and take over. Thank You that You are teaching me to follow Your leadership and to walk in paths of righteousness with You.

⁴ Yea, though I walk through the valley of the shadow of death, I will fear no evil: for thou art with me; thy rod and thy staff they comfort me.

Jesus, thank You that You walk with me through every dark season of life. Thank You Lord that You promised us that the Holy Spirit, our comforter, would always be with us. I turn to You and I am truly sorry for all the times I have turned away from You.

⁵ Thou preparest a table before me in the presence of mine enemies: thou anointest my head with oil; my cup runneth over.

Jesus, thank You that You are there in the midst of every spiritual battle of life! Thank You that You don't abandon us when the battle is raging on. I pray that the anointing of Your presence would fill my heart to overflowing so that Your will would be done.

⁶ Surely goodness and mercy shall follow me all the days of my life: and I will dwell in the house of the Lord forever.

Thank you, Jesus, that You will never leave or abandon us. You are my Good Shepherd and I choose to live for you. Thank You, Jesus, that You give us eternal life and that we will never perish because of what You did for us on the cross. Thank You, Jesus, that no one can snatch us out of Your hand. Amen.

CHAPTER 8

Help My Unbelief!

James knew something about doubt and the devastating impact that it can have on a person's relationship with God. You see, James was one of Jesus' brothers. Not only did he *not* think that Jesus was the Son of God before Jesus' crucifixion and resurrection, but he was convinced that Jesus was crazy. Listen to this encounter that Jesus' family had with Him toward the beginning of his ministry:

> [20] One time Jesus entered a house, and the crowds began to gather again. Soon he and his disciples couldn't even find time to eat. [21] When his family heard what was happening, they tried to take him away. "He's out of his mind," they said. (Mark 3:20-21)

> [31] Then Jesus' mother and brothers came to see him. They stood outside and sent word for him to come out and talk with them. [32] There was a crowd sitting around Jesus, and someone said, "Your mother and your brothers are outside asking for you."

> [33] Jesus replied, "Who is my mother? Who are my

brothers?" [34] Then he looked at those around him and said, "Look, these are my mother and brothers. [35] Anyone who does God's will is my brother and sister and mother." (Mark 3:31-35)

Can you imagine how James must have reacted, hearing Jesus, his brother, say, "Who are my brothers?" But after the resurrection of Jesus, even James became a believer. Now James was the kind of family that Jesus identified Himself with because at long last James was doing the will of God. The dark days of doubt were over and James had become a man of faith. James witnessed firsthand that it is better to obey God the Father than to cater to what pleases others. James learned the hard way that even a person's own family has the potential to get us off track in following the will of God. We are to honor our families, but the ultimate authority in our lives must be the Lord. What made this lesson so intense for James was the fact that he had opposed the will of the Father in Jesus' life. Once we really know that we are sinners saved by the grace of the Lord Jesus Christ, our foolish pretensions and pride have to go. James has much to teach us about how to have victory over doubt and to become men and women of faith.

If our hearts are to move into listening prayer, we have to learn to pray in faith. Our minds want proof of what we are hearing to pray before we pray it aloud. But it doesn't work that way; confirmation of what we pray comes after we pray, not before. Since faith is such an important part of listening prayer, let's allow James to teach us how to overcome our doubts and to move into faith.

Listen to how James starts this letter: "This letter is from James, a slave of God and of the Lord Jesus Christ" (James 1:1). Notice that James didn't try to name-drop and refer to himself as Jesus' brother; instead, James referred to himself as a *slave* of the Lord Jesus Christ. This purity of commitment to Jesus is what doubt will try to steal. Doubt typically takes us out of commission and undermines our commitment to live a life of faith in the Lord Jesus Christ. The first step to overcome doubt is to completely surrender to Jesus' leadership.

John and I had some amazing conversations about faith and the difficulty of overcoming doubt. I told John that faith is like being on the edge of a cliff and then jumping. Recently, I was with friends and students in South Carolina at a cliff where you can jump off into the water below. The cliff was about three stories high, a mere baby jump for serious cliff jumpers. The students and a few other stalwarts like Charlie and Grant immediately began to jump. I, on the other hand, studied the situation. I began to think, "Seriously, I cannot believe that this is happening to me. I hate it when I have to live out my stupid illustrations." Finally, I swam over to the cliff, climbed up to the top of the cliff, and jumped. This is what I told John about cliff jumping and faith: When you are on the edge of a cliff, you can come up with many reasons not to jump. But here is the key to jumping off a cliff: you have to jump.

Since James had actively tried to stop Jesus from living out the will of God the Father, we should take very seriously what James had to say about overcoming doubt and moving into a life of faith.

> [2] Consider it pure joy, my brothers and sisters, whenever you face trials of many kinds, [3] because you know that the testing of your faith produces perseverance. [4] Let perseverance finish its work so that you may be mature and complete, not lacking anything.

> [5] If any of you lacks wisdom, you should ask God, who gives generously to all without finding fault, and it will be given to you. [6] But when you ask, you must believe and not doubt, because the one who doubts is like a wave of the sea, blown and tossed by the wind. [7] That person should not expect to receive anything from the

Lord. [8] Such a person is double-minded and unstable in all they do. (James 1:2-8)

Many people around the world suffer a great deal for following Jesus. The organization Voice of the Martyrs gives present day examples of people who suffer for following Jesus (see persecution.com). Their stories are prime examples of what James meant when he addressed trials. Trials, he said, teach us perseverance. Trials are like refining fire that purifies our faith. James tells us to consider it pure joy when suffering for Jesus, but it's hard to wrap our minds around rejoicing at trials. If we can't yet rejoice, at the very least, his teaching can direct us to look for the hidden blessing of increased faith in the challenges that life brings.

When we pray for someone with listening prayer, in a very real way we ask for God's wisdom to be poured out into someone's heart. Wisdom is the personal application of God's truths for our lives. But if we are to receive this kind of wisdom from the Lord, James tells us that it is important how we ask. When we ask, we must believe and not doubt:

> [5] If you need wisdom, ask our generous God, and he will give it to you. He will not rebuke you for asking. [6] But when you ask him, be sure that your faith is in God alone. Do not waver, for a person with divided loyalty is as unsettled as a wave of the sea that is blown and tossed by the wind. [7] Such people should not expect to receive anything from the Lord. [8] Their loyalty is divided between God and the world, and they are unstable in everything they do. (James 1:5-8 NLT)

In order to believe, we need to purify our hearts from divided loyalties between God and the world. Because of our divided loyalties, we often unknowingly feed doubt. Simple confession before God in Jesus' name that we are guilty is a great place to start. One person described the mental process that he went through with doubt as like being in front of an inquisition table where skeptical questions were raised whenever he tried to move out in faith. St. Augustine taught that understanding comes after faith rather than before faith. You will experience Augustine's insight over and over again as you pray in faith through listening prayer. Sometimes after we pray for people, they will connect the dots for us and tell us why we prayed what we did. When this happens, it is exciting because of the risk of faith that you just took by doing listening prayer. I love what John said: if we knew the answer to every question, then we would be God. Since we are not God, we need to make peace with the fact that not every question will be answered before we are asked to step out in faith. Also, once we realize that the mind justifies what is in the heart, giving our loyalty to Jesus alone will help us defeat the power of doubt in our lives.

James gives us another powerful strategy to increase our faith—we must control our tongue. Since Jesus spoke so powerfully in Mark 11 about the connection between what we say and our faith, it is safe to say that the Holy Spirit inspired James to give emphasis to Jesus' important teaching on increasing our faith. James provides some practical examples to drive his point home about the power and impact of the things we say: a small bit in a horse's mouth controls where the horse goes; a rudder can control the direction of a large ship; and a tiny spark can set a whole forest ablaze. These are each compared to the power of the tongue. Listen to this admonition from James:

> [7] People can tame all kinds of animals, birds, reptiles, and fish, [8] but no one can tame the tongue. It is restless and evil, full of deadly poison. [9] Sometimes it praises our Lord and Father, and sometimes it curses those who have been made in the image of God. [10] And so blessing and cursing come pouring out of the same mouth. Surely, my brothers and sisters, this is not right! [11] Does a spring of water bubble out with

both fresh water and bitter water? ¹² Does a fig tree produce olives, or a grapevine produce figs? No, and you can't draw fresh water from a salty spring. (James 3:7-12)

There are two things we need to do about what we speak. First, we need to stop speaking unbelief and doubt over our ministries. We need to stop speaking against the things that God has said. Secondly, we need to speak in agreement with the Word of God and we need to speak in agreement with the promises that the Lord has given to us. Speaking in agreement with God is a game changer! As crazy as this sounds, we need to listen to the words that come out of our own mouths. It is out of the overflow of the heart that the mouth speaks. When we say things that oppose the Word of God or God's promises for our lives, we need to repent and place what we have said under the blood of Jesus. When we speak against other people's callings from the Lord, we need to repent before God and place what we have said under the blood of Jesus. As James said, how can blessing and cursing come out of the same mouth? When we realize that we are speaking both blessing and cursing out of our mouths, we need to be quick to repent and to put our words under the blood of Jesus.

The final lesson from James concerns putting our faith into practice:

> ¹⁴ What good is it, dear brothers and sisters, if you say you have faith but don't show it by your actions? Can that kind of faith save anyone? ¹⁵ Suppose you see a brother or sister who has no food or clothing, ¹⁶ and you say, "Good-bye and have a good day; stay warm and eat well"—but then you don't give that person any food or clothing. What good does that do?
>
> ¹⁷ So you see, faith by itself isn't enough. Unless it produces good deeds, it is dead and useless.

> [18] Now someone may argue, "Some people have faith; others have good deeds." But I say, "How can you show me your faith if you don't have good deeds? I will show you my faith by my good deeds."
> [19] You say you have faith, for you believe that there is one God-Good for you! Even the demons believe this, and they tremble in terror. [20] How foolish! Can't you see that faith without good deeds is useless? (James 2:14-20 NLT)

Entertaining doubts can move us into inaction in a heartbeat. Doubt can take us down with the paralysis of analysis. James questions whether we have faith if we never produce fruit. I love this statement: "Jesus loves us just the way that we are, but he loves us enough not to leave us the way that we are." We don't do good works to gain our salvation, we do good works as a way of saying thank you for the gift of salvation that is ours through faith in Jesus:

> [8] For it is by grace you have been saved, through faith—and this is not from yourselves, it is the gift of God— [9] not by works, so that no one can boast. [10] For we are God's handiwork, created in Christ Jesus to do good works, which God prepared in advance for us to do. (Eph. 2:8-10)

James ends his strong statements about putting our faith into action by saying that even the demons believe that there is one God. Faith or belief is more than just acknowledging that something is true. Faith is more than mental assent to a truth proposition. Faith is entrusting yourself into the hands of the living God with the heartfelt desire to believe in and follow Jesus. The confession of faith, "Jesus is my Lord and Savior," speaks to the fact that Jesus forgives our sins (He is Savior) and that we proclaim him as the leader (He is Lord) of our lives. This understanding is important for listening prayer. We are called to act upon the things that God speaks to our hearts. It is not enough to learn about listening prayer and never put it into practice. If you read this book and then put it on your shelf or store it on your computer or phone and then never do anything with the practice of listening prayer, you really haven't learned about listening prayer. You learn about listening prayer when you do it.

Do you want an adventure with me or not?

Erica was new to listening prayer and was at a prayer room where she received in prayer to ask the lady next to her if she could pray for her for healing. Erica was reluctant to ask her about this for fear that she was wrong. She sensed the Lord saying to her in prayer, "Do you want an adventure with me or not?" Even though this prayer assignment made her uncomfortable, she decided to move in faith rather than in fear. Erica said that while you would think this would be easy to do because she was in a house of prayer, it was still hard for her to step out in faith. So, Erica asked the lady if she needed healing. The lady asked her if the Lord had told her to ask her this and Erica assured her that He had. They stepped outside to talk. She told Erica that she had nothing physical that needed healing but that she had lost a member of her extended family in a car accident. Erica was able to pray and grieve with her because Erica had been through something similar in her own family. Erica was praising God when she shared this story because of how the Lord had helped her to learn how to step out in faith.

Before we pray, we have no evidence that can possibly satisfy our doubtful minds enough to make us want to pray the things we are receiving to pray. As was said earlier, our minds want proof that what we are hearing in prayer is true before we pray.

Carrie was just moving into listening prayer and she was asked to be a part of a team that helped me pray for college students that were learning about listening prayer. She received something in prayer to give to a student that sounded random to her mind and so she struggled with whether to share it or not. Listen to her story:

Moccasin?

"I was praying for a college student and heard the word moccasin. I had no clue what that meant but remembered Pastor Tim telling me that if I hear something and I don't what it means to just tell the person without an interpretation. So that's what I did. Well, later that evening, the student I prayed for went to a worship night and sat down randomly next to this girl who happened to be wearing moccasins! The student said she knew that God had placed her in that exact seat and that she was supposed to pray for her. The girl wearing the moccasins was really impacted that night."

Our faith gets stronger in listening prayer only after we use it!

One time I heard to pray that what the guy I was praying for had learned with his fists would help him with his calling to do spiritual warfare. When I heard this, on the inside I thought, "I can't pray that, I'm going to offend him." After much internal struggle, I prayed what I had received. After I finished praying, he asked me if I knew what he did for a living. I said, "No, I don't." It turned out he owned a karate studio and that he was a third-degree black belt. I felt shocked and humbled by how much I had resisted praying the words the Holy Spirit had put in my heart. Our minds resist the practice of listening prayer. Your mind wants to protect you from the possibility of looking foolish so it will raise every conceivable doubt about what you are hearing to pray. Doubt will talk you out of ever doing listening prayer if you will let it. But faith gets stronger as you put it into practice. Listening prayer is not something to theorize about but never use.

Having said all of this, I have noticed that after people move into listening prayer that almost to a person they will go through an experience that they don't understand that rocks them to their core. So if you have gone through this, don't let Satan talk you out of continuing to listen to the Lord in prayer. Job finally understood that God thinks differently than we do and that we need to trust the Lord in spite of the fact that we don't understand everything. Just because we don't understand something that has happened, doesn't mean that we are to abandon listening prayer. I was at that crossroads where I was receiving things in prayer that I just did not understand. I will never forget a prayer that I prayed in my car when this lack of understanding was especially intense. I told the Lord that there was a lot about listening prayer that I did not understand but that to the best of my ability I intended to make my decisions for the rest of my life based on what I was receiving from Him in prayer. The Lord spoke to my heart: "I've been waiting to hear you say that." I have never regretted the decision I made. Satan will do everything he can to convince us not to live by being led by the Spirit. Scripture tells us that God's thoughts are above our thoughts (Isa. 55:9). Doubt happens to people who have stepped out in faith, but the doubt doesn't have to take us down the pathway toward unbelief.

John the Baptist boldly proclaimed, "Behold the Lamb of God who takes away the sin of the world" (John 1:29). Listen to this incredible testimony that John the Baptist gave about Jesus' identity as the Son of God:

> 32 Then John (the Baptist) gave this testimony: "I saw the Spirit come down from heaven as a dove and

remain on him. ³³ And I myself did not know him, but the one who sent me to baptize with water told me, 'The man on whom you see the Spirit come down and remain is the one who will baptize with the Holy Spirit.' ³⁴ I have seen and I testify that this is God's Chosen One. (John 1:32-34)

Later, John the Baptist tells the people that he was not the Messiah but he was the one who was sent ahead of the Messiah. John further testified that Jesus must increase and that he must decrease. Finally, John tells the people that there are eternal consequences about what we decide to believe about Jesus: "³⁵ The Father loves the Son and has placed everything in his hands. ³⁶ Whoever believes in the Son has eternal life, but whoever rejects the Son will not see life, for God's wrath remains on them" (John 3:35-36).

But here is the truth of the matter. Sometimes in moments of trauma, pain, and crisis, we question the faith that we once held most dear. You could hardly accuse John the Baptist of not putting his faith into action. So turn the clock ahead. Now John the Baptist has been put in prison and is awaiting execution. John sent some of his disciples to Jesus to ask Jesus if He was the one to come or if they should expect someone else? We don't know for sure what was in John's heart as he asked this question, but it appears that what he was going through had somehow shaken him in his faith. Perhaps he needed reassurance from Jesus that what he had proclaimed was really true. Listen to Jesus' interaction with some of John the Baptist's disciples:

> ¹⁸ John's disciples told him about all these things. Calling two of them, ¹⁹ he sent them to the Lord to ask, "Are you the one who is to come, or should we expect someone else?"
>
> ²⁰ When the men came to Jesus, they said, "John the Baptist sent us to you to ask, 'Are you the one who is

to come, or should we expect someone else?'"

[21] At that very time Jesus cured many who had diseases, sicknesses and evil spirits, and gave sight to many who were blind. [22] So he replied to the messengers, "Go back and report to John what you have seen and heard: The blind receive sight, the lame walk, those who have leprosy are cleansed, the deaf hear, the dead are raised, and the good news is proclaimed to the poor. [23] Blessed is anyone who does not stumble on account of me." (Luke 7:8-23)

Notice what Jesus did to help move John the Baptist, as well as those of us who would come after John the Baptist, from doubt to faith. Jesus gave testimony to the supernatural miracles that He had performed and He presented the evidence of the good news that he was proclaiming to the poor. Testimony about what God the Father is doing through Jesus is still of the utmost importance today if we are to help people move from doubt to faith instead of them moving from doubt to unbelief. Stories of faith moved me away from the tremendous doubt that I had toward myself as well as toward the supernatural events from the Bible.

After my seminary training, doubting Thomas was the disciple I most identified with. Thomas wouldn't believe the report of the resurrection until he could see and touch the risen Jesus himself (John 20:24-29). Amazingly, Jesus allowed this.

Only God and I know I what a miracle it is that I have moved into listening prayer. I would imagine that Thomas would tell you something similar: it was a miracle that Thomas came to believe the resurrection. I will never forget the day when I realized that Jesus' response to Thomas is for all of us that live in this day and time: "Because you have seen me, you have believed; blessed are those who have not seen and yet have believed" (John 20:29).

There is a huge difference between just learning interesting facts and theories about God and really knowing God. During that really difficult season of doubt in my life, I had been working with youth and one of the boys pulled me aside and said, "How do you know God?" I don't remember what I said, but I wasn't happy with my response to his sincere question. My response felt empty. This question has literally stayed with me my whole life. Perhaps this book is an attempt at answering this important question.

It can be difficult to be open to something like God speaking to you if your starting point is a belief that miracles are not possible and that stories having to do with the supernatural are legends. If you believe that God never did miracles even when the Bible was being written, the next step that doubt takes you down is to rip meaning completely out of context and make it say whatever you want it to say. For me, because of feeling lost in a sea of doubt, I needed some reason to believe that the stories the Bible was reporting were true. One day I picked up a Kathryn Kuhlman book about miracles and read about a man crippled from a serious car accident. During the meeting, Kathryn had received a word from the Lord that a man who was crippled from a car accident was being healed and she pointed to the section where this man was sitting. Instantly, he was healed in Jesus' name. I reasoned that if Jesus is still doing things like this today, then miracles happened back then, as well.

However, because of the intensity of the doubt I had gone through around the ministry of the Holy Spirit, I still had to hear story after story about how the Lord speaks today to get past the mountain of skepticism and doubt that had been downloaded into my life, such as the view that those who believe God is still in the supernatural business are just primitive people. I mean, who wants to be thought of as uneducated and primitive? Now, though, I have learned that it doesn't matter what others think. God is awesome and He has not gone on sabbatical! The Holy

Spirit will give you the opportunity to doubt your doubts, if you will let Him!

Having said this, the biggest hurdle of doubt that I had to get past was to accept the biblical worldview that Satan and demons are real. One of Satan's favorite lies today is that he does not exist. If he doesn't exist, then there is no need to resist him. Satan does not want us to learn that we need to resist him—that is why he loves this lie so much. Satan wants no resistance to him putting seeds of doubt in our lives because he doesn't want us to make a complete surrender of ourselves to Jesus. James believed that Satan was real because the devil had definitely played a role in causing him to doubt that Jesus was the Son of God. James tells us to submit to God and that we need to resist the devil so that the devil will flee from us (James 4:7). Once you find out that there really are lying and deceiving spirits, you begin to connect the dots and learn that you need to resist the doubts that Satan tries to send our way. Paul told Timothy that in later times some would abandon their faith because of the influence of lying and deceiving spirits (1 Tim. 4:1). In Genesis 3, we read that Satan deceived Adam and Eve with the question, "Did God really say that you must not eat from the tree in the garden?" Since we know that the cross was the place of Satan's ultimate defeat, it is important to plead the blood of Jesus against doubts that the enemy's camp tries to plant into our lives. Just like war in the natural is real, so spiritual warfare is real.

The following listening prayer story is a reminder of how real the war is. Listen to Matt, in his own words:

Military appointment confirmed

"I was with my friend Hunter and we had just spent the entire day shooting guns on his family farm. All day we had been talking and he was telling me about his background of being raised in a charismatic church and from an early age he was taught that God speaks directly to us.

"During the day he told me how he felt like he had been living his life far from God but that he still felt like he heard the Lord calling him to join the military. He wasn't sure exactly what that was going to look like but he felt very strongly about it.

"Well, I just KNEW this guy was wrong and there was no way he was hearing from God. I had spent months upon months being very hungry to hear the Lord's voice and I was just then beginning to hear Him speak myself. So, there was NO WAY that this guy who admittedly wasn't even really seeking God was hearing from Him.

"Anyways, we went to dinner and continued our discussion about our futures and our faith. During dinner this guy kept saying how God was calling him to the military and confessed he really wanted to be in special operations. Well, now I was irritated and so I was like—I'll just take this guy to get prayed for and see what happens.

"So, I texted Pastor Tim and this was our conversation:

Me: you free

PT: yes

Me: cool if I bring a guy over

PT: come on dude!

"That was it! So, Hunter and I went out to Pastor Tim's to get prayed for. As soon as PT dove into praying for Hunter, he said that there was a strong calling on his life for him to join the military. And PT said he saw him as like a special-ops kind of guy, who could have absolute peace in the face of great trial.

"Well I started freaking out, and after the prayer Hunter was like—you told him about our conversations today? And I was like, No dude. Here, look: this is all I said to the man! And I showed him my texts to Pastor Tim. He

was freaking out like—how did he know!? And I was like dude, he's just confirming what you felt like the Lord was saying to you!"

Dr. Jack Deere came from a background in which he was taught that the supernatural happened long ago but no longer happens today (Cessationism). He called this the problem of the unreal Bible. When you have been taught that God is no longer in the miracle business as the starting point for the interpretation of scripture, the temptation is to only go to the Bible for biblical principles or doctrines. In Deere's book, *Surprised by the Voice of God*, Deere tells his story of moving from the position of being a professor who taught Cessationism to believing that the Holy Spirit is still speaking today. If that is your background and doubt has overwhelmed you that the Holy Spirit still speaks, you might want to read Deere's book. It helped me tremendously in my search for what the Bible teaches about hearing from the Lord in prayer.

Sometimes we tend to think of doubt as a neutral position between faith and unbelief, but it's really not. It is probably more accurate to see doubt as an attack on our faith. It is really a short step from doubt to unbelief. After Jesus had been raised from the dead, the gospel of Matthew tells us that some of the disciples doubted. The gospel of Mark records this interaction that Jesus had with his doubting disciples:

> [9] When Jesus rose early on the first day of the week, he appeared first to Mary Magdalene, out of whom he had driven seven demons. [10] She went and told those who had been with him and who were mourning and weeping. [11] When they heard that Jesus was alive and that she had seen him, they did not believe it. [12] Afterward Jesus appeared in a different form to two of them while they were walking in the country. [13] These

returned and reported it to the rest; but they did not believe them either. [14] Later Jesus appeared to the Eleven as they were eating; he rebuked them for their lack of faith and their stubborn refusal to believe those who had seen him after he had risen. (Mark 16:9-14)

The disciples all went to their death proclaiming the gospel as they told people about how faith in Jesus as the Son of God changes everything. However, doubt almost took them down before they ever got started. Jesus rebuked them for doubting the testimony of others that He was raised from the dead. Why would Jesus give them a strong rebuke for this? Jesus knew that it wouldn't be long before they would be the ones giving their testimony about Jesus as the Son of God and that they had seen Him raised from the dead! He confronted them because they were going to need to be strong in their faith—strong enough to be able to confront others about the truth of the gospel even in the face of horrific unbelief. Don't live in fear of the Lord's rebuke! Welcome it: it will strengthen you to do the will of God through your life so that Jesus will get all the glory and honor and praise for what the Holy Spirit does through your life!

> *Dear Lord, I confess that at times I have been paralyzed by doubt. I place my loyalty in You alone, O God. Thank You, Lord, that You are strengthening my faith in the supernatural ministry of the Holy Spirit. Thank You, Lord, for making me strong in my faith so that others will come to know Jesus as Savior and Lord. In Jesus' name, I pray. Amen.*

CHAPTER 9

Having the Humility of Christ

Members of our team were headed to Arizona to lead a listening prayer conference for a local church. As Kelli was walking through a coffee shop area at the Chicago airport, I saw her stop at a table and speak to the lady sitting there. Kelli told her that she was learning to listen to Jesus' voice and that she wanted to tell her that she felt like Jesus wanted to do something amazing for children through her life. The lady told her, "I am a child psychologist." They then shared a short but meaningful conversation. I love how Kelli's humble approach created a "woman at the well" type of encounter with Jesus. No matter how long we have been hearing Jesus' voice, we are all always still learning in listening prayer.

In chapter seven, we studied the serious unbelief James overcame. He became one of the early leaders in the church because he opened the door of his heart to let Jesus take over his life. James models how to get close to God. He shows us the importance of humbling ourselves before the Lord in prayer:

> [5] Do you think the Scriptures have no meaning? They say that God is passionate that the spirit he has placed

within us should be faithful to him. ⁶ And he gives grace generously. As the Scriptures say,

> "God opposes the proud
> but gives grace to the humble."

⁷ So humble yourselves before God. Resist the devil, and he will flee from you. ⁸ Come close to God, and God will come close to you. Wash your hands, you sinners; purify your hearts, for your loyalty is divided between God and the world. ⁹ Let there be tears for what you have done. Let there be sorrow and deep grief. Let there be sadness instead of laughter, and gloom instead of joy. ¹⁰ Humble yourselves before the Lord, and he will lift you up in honor. (James 4:5-10 NLT)

The importance of humbling ourselves before God in order to draw close to Him is mentioned in this passage over and over again. Human nature being what it is, we love attention and being thought of as a cut above the rest. We are trained to compete and want to be the best at everything we do. In Genesis, we read that Satan successfully tempted Adam and Eve to fall into sin through an appeal for them to be like God. Our pride knows no end. It is no wonder scripture reminds us repeatedly about the importance of humbling ourselves before God. Pride is toxic to our relationships with people and to our relationship with the Lord. What makes pride so difficult to deal with is that often we don't know that we have it. When God reveals something extraordinary through listening prayer, we need to be impressed with the Lord rather than with the one who is praying the prayer. There is nothing that will derail listening prayer quicker than allowing it to feed pride, ours or someone else's.

One day I asked Jean (name changed) if I could pray for her. I took a second to humble myself out loud as well as plead the blood of Jesus over the prayer time. Before I started praying specifically for Jean, I received in prayer that I hadn't humbled myself enough. I didn't understand because I thought my heart was in a humble place, but, regardless, I got really serious about humbling myself out loud before the Lord before I prayed for her at all. When I finished the time of listening prayer, I was totally surprised by the response. Jean said that she had never wanted to hear another word of knowledge prayer for the rest of her life because of the pride she had encountered when others prayed specific words for her previously. She said that because I had humbled myself, she was able to listen to the word of knowledge that was in the prayer. Jean's reaction put the fear of the Lord in me. We must carefully guard our hearts against pride because it always crouches at our door (Genesis 4:6). Before we pray for someone, we need to humble ourselves before God. After we pray for someone, we need to humble ourselves before God.

James explains that we need to purify our hearts because our loyalty is divided between God and the world. If our motivation is to impress someone by what we pray for them, we have set ourselves up to get off track with the Lord. As the Holy Spirit seeks to teach us how to listen in prayer, lingering pride can hinder us from hearing clearly from the Lord. If we want to hear a specific word in order to feel important, to feel better about ourselves, or out of a performance mentality, it is time to repent and humble ourselves before the Lord.

Brittany's testimony is helpful at this point:

Gift exchange

"For three years or so, I have volunteered with a ministry that focuses on praying for the sick in addition to listening prayer. One night, we were there and things were going at a decent pace when our next visitor entered. She was a pre-teen and, admittedly, there was somewhat of a generational gap. Whereas I wasn't quite old enough to be more than a big sister, the others were probably around the ages of her

grandparents and she seemed quite underwhelmed to be in our company. After a brief prayer, the others ministered to her. She wasn't very responsive. 'What could I possibly say to this little girl to get this sour look off her face?' I asked God. Then, I saw a picture that I initially encountered on social media months prior. In the picture, there was a very little girl standing in front of Jesus. Jesus' right hand was extended to her as He said, 'Just trust me...,' but she couldn't take His hand because she was holding onto a small teddy bear in front of her with both hands, saying, 'But I love it, God...' Little did she know that Jesus had a gift for her in His left hand, hidden behind His back. It was a much larger, newer teddy bear that she wouldn't be able to enjoy until she surrendered what she had.

"When I mentioned this to the pre-teen in front of me at the table, she immediately perked up and engaged us in prayer because she had just seen that picture earlier in the day! Immediately, we were able to touch, agree, and listen together. The atmosphere was changed!"

"This experience is still a sweet memory to me concerning listening prayer because it reminds me how God uses the simplest things to help us encourage one another and edify the body of Christ. Since then, I've spoken more boldly and courageously... I leave the 'spectacular' part to Him. Whether I think the picture I see is 'trivial' or not, I do not underestimate the power of God to communicate effectively in whatever way He chooses."

☙

What Brittany has said illustrates that listening prayer is about Jesus, not about us. The Lord is in charge of what we hear, not us. If we are truly humble before the Lord, we will no longer care if we look impressive or not. There are people I know who hear and share more specific details than I typically receive in prayer. My response? "Yay, Jesus! I am so glad that You use other people in greater ways than You use me to reveal how much You love people!"

When we disciple people in listening prayer, the hope needs to be that the people that we influence will be used in much greater ways than we are. I recently met with a group who were asking the Holy Spirit to teach us how to receive even more specific words for people so that they would come to know Jesus as the Son of God. We asked the Holy Spirit to teach us so that the people that we pray for would have experiences like the woman at the well when Jesus told her that she had been married five times and the one that she was now with was not her husband. Listening prayer's purpose is to reveal Jesus as the Son of God, share his love, and to walk in humility and obedience before God. When we really are humble, rather than when we just try to look humble, the Lord can use us in incredible ways to help bring prodigal sons and daughters home to him.

One night after a student social gathering, the Lord spoke to my heart that I had been showing off in front of the students. I knew instantly that it was true. I felt so embarrassed. I asked the hard question, "Lord, what do you want me to do about it?" I heard in prayer that I needed to confess the next day in my Sunday morning message that I had been showing off in front of students the night before. I needed to confess publicly, because when I was showing off, it was done publicly. I also heard in prayer that many would repent before the Lord about their own sin once I confessed my pride. Public confession was hard for me to accept, because my pride was resisting being humbled like that. The good news is that after I had confessed my pride, the altar was filled with students repenting before God for their own pride.

Humility is fine to talk about as long as we don't have to do it. Our pride gives us a thousand self-justifying reasons why we don't have to humble ourselves before God and others. *Hey*, it tells us, *I humbled myself when I got saved, no need to ever humble myself like that again!* Once you have invited the Holy

Spirit to speak to you and to lead and guide you in your life, you have opened yourself up to correction. But we can be assured Jesus corrects us because He loves us. Jesus said,

> [1]I am the True Vine, and My Father is the Vinedresser.[2] Any branch in Me that does not bear fruit [that stops bearing] He cuts away (trims off, takes away); and He cleanses and repeatedly prunes every branch that continues to bear fruit, to make it bear more and richer and more excellent fruit. (John 15:1-2 AMP)

When we let the Holy Spirit speak to us, we invite Jesus' pruning into our lives so that we will bear even more fruit.

I had received in prayer that I was supposed to go for an interview for a campus ministry position even though I would not be chosen for the job. I had been on a couple of similar interviews over the course of a few years. I had received in prayer that I was supposed to go to these interviews to be a witness even though I would not be chosen for the positions. I told a friend about how I was complaining to the Lord about not wanting to go experience yet another interview like this. My friend said, "You sound like Jonah." I said, "I do sound like Jonah, don't I!" That same morning, I led a time of listening prayer for students and had the opportunity to pray for an awesome student. When I finished praying, I received in prayer to ask her if she would pray for me. She said, "Pastor Tim, I don't know what this means to you but I feel like the Lord wants me to remind you of the story of Jonah?" I threw my hands up in the air, dropped to my knees, and I said very loudly, "Stop praying! God, I repent and I will go to this interview with a good attitude and I will be a witness for you." After I humbled myself before the Lord, the Lord's presence on my life for that full day-long interview was amazing. At the interview, I witnessed to folks about how real Jesus is through listening prayer. So many wonderful things happened that day even though I did not get the job. I am so thankful that God loves us enough to correct us and prune us so that we will bear even more fruit.

Jeannie and Grant had been asked to pray for a group of pastors. Listen to what happened.

Scary prayer that's not so scary

"We were invited to minister prayer to pastors at a retreat. Many were very open and stood in line for prayer. The Lord spoke to each in very personal ways. There was a dear man, an older pastor, who had been in the ministry many years and he told us that he was a little bit scared about experiencing listening prayer. We assured him that it was okay and asked for the Holy Spirit to speak to him. It was just such an honor to see how the Lord loved him. After we finished praying, we asked him, 'That wasn't so scary after all, was it?' Much to our amusement, he replied, 'No, but it was still a bit scary!'"

Since my father was a pastor, and I have been a pastor my whole adult life, I can testify that sometimes as a pastor you feel like you are supposed to know all about the Bible and all things spiritual. When I was in college, I was a fill-in pastor for two months. One of my fears was that someone would ask me where something was in the Bible and that I wouldn't know where it was. Since I had really just started reading my Bible, I figured I was toast. I visited a lady in her nineties and she asked me right at the beginning of the visit, "Where is it in the Bible where Jesus first called his disciples?" I quickly said, "John 1." This just happened to be the scripture passage that I would be preaching on that week. It was the only scripture passage that I would have known the location for at that moment in time. I told a friend of mine about what happened and he said that he knew where the Ten Commandments were but that was about the only thing he knew. I asked him where the Ten Commandments were in the Bible and he told me Exodus 20. The following week I went to visit this same lady and she said, "Preacher, I want to ask you where something is in the Bible?" I instantly knew that I was about to fail her Bible test and that the church was probably going to have to give me the old heave-ho, out the door I go. She said, "Where are the Ten Commandments in the Bible?" I quickly said that they were in Exodus 20. She was finally convinced that I was a Bible expert so this was the last time that she asked me a question like this.

Pastors, you don't have to be an expert at everything. Humility is a good thing and it will take humility to be open to moving into something like listening prayer if it has been foreign to your experience. Even if you are in the later years of your ministry, I can't think of a better time for a new beginning! Why not plan on learning new things about the Lord right up until He takes us home? I applaud those of you who have been willing to be open to listening prayer, especially if is outside of the religious tradition you grew up with. Experiencing listening prayer was outside of the religious tradition I grew up with, but I am so glad that I said yes to the Lord rather than no to moving into knowing Him like this.

Janet was in high school at the time when I was first introduced to the power of the Holy Spirit and listening prayer. I could see that she knew the Lord in ways that I did not. Pastors, lay down your pride and be willing to learn from others even if they are much younger than you! Remember how Paul told Timothy not to despise his youth? In other words, Timothy, you know the Lord and even people who are older than you will be so blessed to learn about following Jesus from you! Janet was a great teacher. She patiently explained things to me about the Holy Spirit. So, pastors, it is a good thing to humble yourselves before others and before God. Why not be willing to lay down the facade that you are an expert on all things spiritual and be willing to learn about listening prayer if this is new to you?

One of the best places to learn about humility and faith is from children:

> At that time the disciples came to Jesus and asked, "Who, then, is the greatest in the kingdom of heaven?" [2] He called a little child to him, and placed the child among them. [3] And he said: "Truly I tell you, unless you change and become like little children, you will never enter the kingdom of heaven. [4] Therefore, whoever takes the lowly position of this child is the greatest in the kingdom of heaven. [5] And whoever welcomes one such child in my name welcomes me. (Matt. 18:1-5)

I have had the privilege of being in meetings where middle school students are crying out to God. Seeing a seventh grader crying out to God from the bottom of his heart is incredibly humbling; it will change you. Some of the greatest blessings you will ever receive happen when children pray for you. Five and six year olds who love Jesus pray with the kind of childlike faith that Jesus wants adults to have. One day a five-year-old little girl prayed for me and her prayer sent me weeping to the feet of Jesus. It is humbling and freeing to realize that small children have so much to teach us! Here is the wonderful miracle of childlike-faith: at the Brownsville revival, I witnessed people who were hardened by the world get childlike innocence restored in a baptismal pool. One night I helped baptize a guy who had a hardened shell because of the way he had lived, but he had a deep childlike faith on the inside. Jesus specializes in coming to live on the inside and giving people a brand-new life!

And a little child shall lead them

Once a mom asked me if I would help her move into listening prayer. Her 9-year-old daughter was with her. I said "Sure, but if you would, just listen in while I talk to your daughter." I took ten minutes to explain to her about listening to God.

I told her, "I know that when you look at me you are thinking, 'He is really old.' But guess what, when I pray, I am your age. You are the perfect age to listen to the Lord." After that, I asked her to listen in prayer and pray for me. She started to say something, but hesitated. I said, "What is it?" She said, tentatively, "Jesus is giving you righteousness?" I took out my phone, opened my Bible memory app, and showed her the Bible verse I had been studying that week. "Blessed are those who hunger and thirst for righteousness, for they shall be filled." I asked, "Did you know that I have been looking at this verse all week?" She said, "No." I told her, "Jesus knew I was looking at that verse."

ﷺ

One evening I was with a group of college students in an apartment right by their university. A twelve-year-old boy was with his sister. I took a few minutes to explain listening prayer to him. He started praying for college students, and then the next thing we knew, college students were sitting in line to get prayed for by a 12-year-old boy. People were getting their worlds rocked as they received prayer. I was sitting with a guy who was shaking his head the whole time the boy prayed for him. The 12-year-old said to the 23-year-old, "I hope that meant something to you." The 23-year-old replied, "You just prayed the prayer I pray every morning." The 23-year-old sat on the floor, leaned up against a wall, and shook his head for the next half hour or so.

ﷺ

While we want to have childlike faith to move into listening prayer, we don't want to be childish in our character. There are many character lessons that we need to learn as we are learning to listen to the Lord in prayer. The best person to teach us all about character is Jesus! The Apostle Paul knew this and told us that we need to have the attitude of Christ. Before we listen to the Lord in prayer, we need to put Jesus' mantle of humility on so that we can move into the character, attitude, and mind of Christ. Once we have prayed through listening prayer, we need to make sure that we continue to live in the humility and attitude of Christ. The Apostle Paul had to learn this the hard way. He thought he had his faith completely figured out until he met Jesus on the Damascus Road. After Paul had been severely humbled, he was finally in a place where the Lord could use him. Listen to what Paul had to say to a group of young Christians about the importance of learning to be humble the way that Jesus was:

> [1]Is there any encouragement from belonging to Christ? Any comfort from his love? Any fellowship together in the Spirit? Are your hearts tender and compassionate? [2] Then make me truly happy by agreeing wholeheartedly with each other, loving one another, and working together with one mind and purpose. [3] Don't be selfish; don't try to impress others. Be humble, thinking of others as better than yourselves. [4] Don't look out only for your own interests, but take an interest in others, too. [5] You must have the same attitude that Christ Jesus had.

> [6] Though he was God,
>   he did not think of equality with God
>   as something to cling to.
> [7] Instead, he gave up his divine privileges;
>   he took the humble position of a slave
>   and was born as a human being.
>   When he appeared in human form
> [8] he humbled himself in obedience to God
>   and died a criminal's death on a cross.
> [9] Therefore, God elevated him to the place of highest

honor and gave him the name above all other names,
¹⁰ that at the name of Jesus every knee should bow,
in heaven and on earth and under the earth,
¹¹ and every tongue declare that Jesus Christ is Lord,
to the glory of God the Father. (Phil. 1:1-11)

But, you wonder, how in the world can I make the humility of Jesus a reality in my life? I don't think that I can pull this off. You are right: in our own strength, we cannot make this happen. For heaven's sake, we will even become prideful about how humble we are! The way that we can begin to walk in the humility of Jesus is to do life together with Jesus:

> ²⁸ Come to me, all you who are weary and burdened, and I will give you rest. ²⁹ Take my yoke upon you and learn from me, for I am gentle and humble in heart, and you will find rest for your souls. ³⁰ For my yoke is easy and my burden is light. (Matt. 11:28-30)

On a recent trip through Pennsylvania, I saw horse carriages on the road in the midst of heavy traffic. Without proper training, most horses cannot tolerate the noise and chaos of cars whizzing by. To train them to focus calmly and trust the carriage driver, a young horse will be yoked with an older horse that is not alarmed at having cars fly past. The older horse is there to teach the younger horse to follow the lead of the person holding the reins. When we are yoked to Jesus, we can begin to learn to follow the leadership of the Holy Spirit.

In his letter to the Colossians, Paul reveals the secret of living for the Lord is "Christ in you, the hope of glory." Once we realize that we are sons and daughters of the King, and that it is Jesus who is doing the work in us and through us, there is no room for pride. Thankfully the Lord loves us enough to correct us when we get off track because we have forgotten who we are. So, what do you think? Yeah, pride is overrated! Why don't we lay down our pride and humble ourselves before the Lord in prayer?

Dear Lord, I want to live for You, Jesus, rather than for myself. I humble myself before You, Lord, and I lay down my know-it-all, prideful attitude at Your feet. Teach me to move in childlike faith, Jesus, so that You will get all the glory for what You do through my life! In Jesus' name, I pray. Amen.

CHAPTER 10

From Fear to Faith

When we are hijacked by fear, it is difficult to hear from the Lord in prayer. We are afraid of what people think and we are often afraid of looking foolish or like a failure in front of others. It is scary how much we worry about what others think about us. We don't limit ourselves to people we know, either: we worry about what complete strangers think about us. It's as if our identity as individuals is held hostage by how the world judges us. Yet if we are serious about getting close to God through listening prayer, our self-conscious mentality has to change. When our focus is to get right with the Lord, and to live in a way that pleases Him, we are set free to become the men and women God has created us to be. But when the foremost desire in our hearts is to please those closest to us, it can block what the Lord wants to say to us.

How can we prevent the fear of what others think about us from blocking us in hearing from the Lord? The place to start to get victory in this area is to care more about what God thinks rather than about what people think. We need to take these verses from Isaiah to heart:

> [12] I, even I, am he who comforts you.
>   Who are you that you fear mere mortals,
>   human beings who are but grass,
> [13] that you forget the LORD your Maker,
>   who stretches out the heavens
>   and who lays the foundations of the earth,
>   that you live in constant terror every day
>   because of the wrath of the oppressor,
>   who is bent on destruction? (Isa. 51:12-13)

You might think, I see what you are saying here, but letting go of fear is easier said than done. So here is the question: how do we learn to live in faith rather than in fear? It must have been incredible being one of Jesus' original disciples, watching Jesus open blind eyes, heal lepers, and raise the dead. Imagine how difficult it was for these disciples to hear Jesus say that it was a good thing for Him to go away. Really? How could this possibly be a good thing? Jesus told them that unless He went away the Holy Spirit would not come to them:

> [4b] I did not tell you this from the beginning because I was with you, [5] but now I am going to him who sent me. None of you asks me, 'Where are you going?' [6] Rather, you are filled with grief because I have said these things. [7] But very truly I tell you, it is for your good that I am going away. Unless I go away, the Advocate will not come to you; but if I go, I will send him to you. (John 16:4b-7)

At the time the disciples probably had no clue what Jesus was talking about. They could never have imagined the fear that they were about to go through right after Jesus told them this, but the Holy Spirit coming to them was of the utmost importance. Possibly for them, at that moment in time, and as well as for many of us, the Holy Spirit seemed a concept to be understood rather than a partnership to be lived out. So how do we transition from having only intellectual knowledge of a theoretical spiritual being, to having a relationship with the person of the Holy Spirit? What needs to change in us so that our lives will have maximum impact for the Kingdom of God? What we need to learn is what the first disciples were to learn: the job that Jesus gave them to do would be impossible without the power and leadership of the Holy Spirit in their lives.

After Jesus was crucified, the disciples hid behind locked doors. Their security was threatened and the possibility of bodily harm seemed imminent. How could they overcome this crippling fear? Fast forward to the 18th century, when John Wesley, founder of the Methodist church, was on a ship and it looked like the passengers and crew of whole ship were going to perish in the storm. A group of Moravians on board the ship were praying and were in perfect peace, even in the face of death. Their absolute assurance of their salvation and their faith in eternal life in the face of the imminent possibility of death caused John Wesley to think: they know something that I don't know.

After the disciples encountered Jesus after God raised Him from the dead, the tables were turned in the enemy's camp. The risen Christ instructed them to wait for power from on high. The disciples gathered together constantly to pray and continued to pray until the fire of God fell from heaven. To move into all the assignments that God has for us, we desperately need the power of the Holy Spirit in our lives. We need the kind of courage that can only come from the Holy Spirit. The Holy Spirit is what we need to move us from fear to faith.

There is part of us that longs to connect with God in a deep personal way, yet there is also part of us that is afraid to do this for fear of what might happen. We think, "There has got to be more to life than this!" But what we have to learn to do is to take risks of faith even though everything within us resists.

The first risky thing we are called to is to say yes to the Holy Spirit's leadership in our lives. If you have been resisting saying yes to whatever the Holy Spirit wants to do in your life, why not go for it and say, "Yes, Lord!" No matter what you've experienced in the Lord, there is more, and the key to moving forward is to move forward in faith! However, that's easier said than done for most people. Once we decide to get serious about moving outside of our comfort zone, we will desperately need spiritual help from the Lord. So why not take a moment right now and pray, "I ask, Lord, for the power, the fire, and the leadership of the Holy Spirit to come into my life so that I will have the power to be a witness for Jesus. I ask You to do in my life, Lord, whatever You choose to do!"

At a rehearsal dinner for a wedding I performed in Atlanta, Mary Lou told me that she prays every day, "Fill me more with you Jesus." As we partner at deeper and deeper levels with the Holy Spirit, we need to ask Jesus to live His life through us more and more. The following verses that Paul wrote under the leadership of the Holy Spirit remind me of the prayer that Mary Lou loves to pray:

> [20] I have been crucified with Christ and I no longer live, but Christ lives in me. The life I now live in the body, I live by faith in the Son of God, who loved me and gave himself for me. (Gal. 2:20)

> [27] To them God has chosen to make known among the Gentiles the glorious riches of this mystery, which is Christ in you, the hope of glory. (Col. 1:27)

> [16] I pray that out of his glorious riches he may strengthen you with power through his Spirit in your inner being, [17] so that Christ may dwell in your hearts through faith. (Eph. 3:16-17a)

We need to say *yes* to Jesus living His life through our lives. When we do this, Jesus starts replacing our fears with His life of faith. Why not say *yes* to Jesus taking over and to the Holy Spirit filling us up to overflowing with the love of Jesus? When people are first moving into listening prayer, they are often shocked at the fears they need to overcome to pray this way. Jacquelyn and her husband were newlyweds in two challenging jobs and going to school full time. In the midst of all this, they signed up for a listening prayer class. It was hard for them to hear from the Lord with all the chaos in their lives. She and her husband went to the first prayer class and got intrigued, curious, and hungry for the Lord.

Beginning to listen

In Jacquelyn's own words, "Before our second class, I was in my room, crying and praying for the Lord to hear me. I told the Holy Spirit that I planned on asking Pastor Tim to do this 'Listening Prayer' over me once our class ended that day. Wouldn't you know, in the middle of his teaching, he stops and goes, 'I don't normally do this, but is there a volunteer willing for me to demonstrate and pray for them?' My heart immediately went from 'Oh, hi there, I'm chillin',' to 'Oh my gosh, where am I? Get me out of here!!!' I thought to myself, 'Oh no, Holy Spirit. Please don't do this. I don't want to raise my hand.' Next thing I know my hand is barely in the air. PT scans the room, as there are several people with their hands up. He looks directly at me. My heart is racing, 'Please no, please no, please no,' and next thing I know, it's game over for my comfort zone. I hear, 'You, can I pray for you?' What I didn't know until later is that the Holy Spirit had highlighted me to PT, which is why I got picked. Needless to say, I bawled almost the whole time, first, because the Holy Spirit heard me in my room for what seemed like the first time in a very long time, second, because PT prayed so much life into several broken situations I had been going through that he knew nothing about."

For Jacquelyn, it was a huge breakthrough to get past the fear barrier and receive listening prayer in front of those people. The next fear barrier that she had to fight her way through was when it was time for her to start praying out loud for another person what she was hearing in prayer. Months later she was paired up with a student from campus and she began to take the risk of praying the things she was receiving. Again, in Jacquelyn's words, "During the prayer I saw math, like a ruler, numbers, equations, etc., but it was weird because when I went to tell her, all that came out was: 'Algebra.' She immediately started crying. The next vision I got was of her and a boy. So, I said, 'Boy.' And she cried even harder. I couldn't tell you what other words I got or if we even finished praying, because those words impacted her beyond anything I was expecting. She had been feeling like she was suffocating in her algebra class for some time now, and she was in a crossroads situation with a boy. Both were extremely major events in her life and yet, both extremely different subjects. It was in that moment when I quietly whispered to myself that that was it. I was going to pursue this for the rest of my life."

Once you see the love of Jesus touch someone, the walls of fear that we have built up around ourselves come tumbling down. Like Jacquelyn, you might decide to pursue listening prayer for the rest of your life. Jesus' perfect love really does cast out fear. As you begin to move into listening in prayer for others, you will be shocked at how much Jesus really does love people. Once you get a glimpse of the way that Jesus loves people, it changes how you see them. You no longer see them as people that hold your identity hostage but as people that Jesus died for on the cross.

When our Campus Thirst team first helps people to listen to

the Holy Spirit, we get people in a circle, put one person in the middle, and practice listening for that person for just one word, or a phrase, or for a picture we see on the inside. When people first begin doing this, we help them fight their fear. People will receive things in prayer but will not share what they are receiving because of fear. Finally, after time and practice, people start to get more comfortable with listening to the Holy Spirit and praying for people they know. Once this starts to feel a little bit like a comfort zone, it's time to move people further out of their comfort zones and in to praying for strangers.

I first prayed for Tim in a prayer outreach on a university campus. I prayed that he would be an evangelist on campus and see signs and wonders in his ministry. When Tim heard this prayer, it seemed impossible to him because even thinking about talking to other students on campus about Jesus filled him with fear. Tim's initial response to what I prayed for him would certainly have been my response if someone had prayed something like that for me.

I was on an airplane some years back and felt like I needed to offer to pray for the guy next to me. The fear I felt was crippling. I've always known that I have lived far below what I could be doing for the Great Commission because of the way I have let fear talk me out of sharing my faith. I often wondered, how do I get past this seemingly all-consuming fear of what people think? Finally, I offered to pray for the guy next to me and he said yes. After praying for him, I tried to witness some. All at once my ridiculous fear struck me as funny, so I told the guy, "Hey, I guess you can tell that I'm trying to witness to you. I'm not very good at it; I'm sorry." He said, "Oh no, you're doing fine, you're doing fine!" I found out that his sister was a pastor's wife and it hit me what I've always heard Bill say: it's amazing that sometimes we get to be the answer to someone's prayers.

So, let's get back to Tim's story. The Lord has done such a miracle in Tim's life. Now, Tim is one of the boldest people I have ever known. What happened? Tim heard the evangelist Todd

White speak about how fear of what other people think can be left behind once we realize how loved we are by Jesus and how much Jesus loves the people that we are offering to minister to. Tim believed this and was immediately off-the-chart bold! One evening during finals week, we were in a public eating area on a university campus when Tim started going table to table to invite students to our table to be prayed for. I asked Tim if he had ever done that before, and he said, "No, never!" It was amazing to watch him walk up to tables of complete strangers and invite them to come to our table for prayer. On one of the nights, there was a line to our table that extended the full length of the eating area. It was incredible, and Tim and I were officially launched into praying for students on campus. I could never have imagined 16 years prior to this that my college ministry building would one day be a sidewalk. It's a church without walls.

That first fall started with us going to an event called "campsite." Groups were camped out on the sidewalk to get basketball tickets and Tim walked up to every group and said, "Hey, I've got my friend Pastor Tim here with me. Would it be ok to encourage you guys by letting him pray for you?" The groups were all close together so lots of folks got to see us headed their way before we even got to them. Many of the males rolled their eyes when wives and moms agreed, with a little too much enthusiasm, for me to pray for the group. One guy sought us out later and thanked us for praying for his sister. He said that he had been witnessing to her for some time and he appreciated what we were doing. After it was over, I asked Tim if approaching the groups to offer prayer had made him uncomfortable. After thinking about it, he said, "No, not really." I told him, "I thought so. *I* was really uncomfortable!" Our challenge is to learn how to become comfortable with being uncomfortable. Four and five days a week we would stand outside on campus and offer to pray for people as they walked by. The number of people we touched that year was in the thousands. Now Tim has an incredible street ministry, and yes, he has gotten to see signs and wonders out on the street. And yes, he has led people to receive Jesus as Lord and to become born again, the greatest miracle of all!

When we take teams out on university campuses to pray for people, the biggest surprise for new people going out to pray is how peaceful and chill the whole event is. Teams are often shocked at how many people say *yes* to the offer of prayer. However, what often stands out the most to those who walk around with us are the people who say *no* to our offer to pray for them. Some politely say *no*, some say *no* with varying degrees of disdain, but some say *no* with hostility and anger. We do our best to respond with kindness and humility to every *no* we receive. I share with the new people who go out with us that those who give a harsh *no* are people that we especially love to touch with the love of Jesus. Our desire is to connect with folks who would be highly unlikely to ever consider going to a church. After treating the people who have said *no* with respect, regardless of how strongly they say it, we will stand there and pray for them after they have walked away. Once you realize that the person you are praying for could become the next Apostle Paul, it changes your attitude and helps your faith triumph over your fear!

Being around other people who are moving in faith rather than fear is exciting. Josh went up to a large group who were sitting on the ground in the center of his university campus. A couple of the students in the group let Josh and others pray for them. I had walked by the group earlier and had felt somewhat intimidated to ask them if a couple of us could pray for them. What Josh and his group did was so inspiring to me that the next day when I saw a group of guys sitting at a table in the restaurant we were eating at, I started praying and listening in prayer for what I could do for them. I got in prayer to walk up to the table of guys and thank them for being men of God. After I shared that word, they hopped up and wanted to take a picture with me. I got to pray for all of them. One had just been baptized that morning. The guy who wanted to take the picture was preparing for the ministry, and when I asked him if I could pray for him, he said, "Do what you do!" The exciting part for me was to hear their hunger for revival on campus. All of this was happening in the middle of a restaurant! The folks that worked there took all of it in with curiosity. Before I went to the guys' table, I was sitting at a table of young adults and Laura said, "Stop! Let's watch: PT is praying and staring at that table back there. Something is getting ready to go down!" Here I am in my 60s and have never done things like this in my entire life. Being around students who are in love with Jesus and willing to live in faith rather than in fear has been a huge inspiration!

Go!

A group of five Chinese students walked by a couple of us on the way to the library on campus. One of the students in our group said, "I think I was supposed to pray for them." This student had lit a fire under me earlier when she saw me hesitate to ask a guy that had just walked by if I could pray for him. She was behind me and said, "Go!" After a quick step or two, I was able to catch up to him and had a great time of prayer. Now it was my turn: I said, "Go!" This student took off running and intercepted the group before they went into the library, and the four guys and one girl let her pray for each one of them. They asked her if they should fold their hands or what they were supposed to do when she prayed. She said, "You can just stand there while I pray for you." We look right at folks when we pray for them in those kinds of settings. It's powerful praying this way! Each of the five hugged her when she was finished praying for them all. Her joyous countenance and her prayers had touched them.

The Apostle Paul was an amazing Spirit-led witness for the Lord Jesus Christ. Even in the midst of conflicts, he was always teaching people how important it is to have the right heart before God. Let these words of Paul inspire you to move from living to please people to living to please the Lord:

> [6] I am astonished that you are so quickly deserting the one who called you to live in the grace of Christ and are turning to a different gospel— [7] which is really no gospel at all. Evidently some people are throwing you into confusion and are trying to pervert the gospel of Christ. [8] But even if we or an angel from heaven should preach a gospel other than the one we preached to you, let them be under God's curse! [9] As we have already said, so now I say again: If anybody is preaching to you a gospel other than what you accepted, let them be under God's curse!
>
> [10] Am I now trying to win the approval of human beings, or of God? Or am I trying to please people? If I were still trying to please people, I would not be a servant of Christ. (Gal. 1:6-10)

So, what do you think, are you ready for faith to win out over fear? Are you willing to say to the Lord that you want to please Him rather than to just be about pleasing people? Are you ready to take the risk of faith and ask the Lord to speak to you in listening prayer?

Dear Lord, I confess that I have often moved in fear rather than in faith. I have allowed the fear of what others might think stop me from being a witness for Jesus. Lord, the desire of my heart is to please You with my life rather than just to please people. I lay my fears down before You, Jesus, and I ask You, Lord, to fill me with the Holy Spirit. In Jesus' name, I pray. Amen.

CHAPTER 11

Adventure Awaits

So, I was getting ready to take a group of students out on a university campus and was feeling a little nervous because this was my first time at this particular campus. I've learned when I feel like this that getting a good *no* is exactly what I need to get going. We weren't even on campus yet and I was barely out of the car when I saw him. I thought, "There's a good *no*, for sure." The dude was 6'2," with big black hair and a huge black beard. "So excuse me, man, I'm Pastor Tim and we are just trying to encourage people by praying for them. Could I pray for you real quick?" He said, "Uh, NO!" As we walked past each other, the whole thing struck me as really funny. I turned back to look at him and he turned back look at me at the exact same moment in time. We both reached out, tapped each other on the arm, and both of us walked away laughing. You know he was thinking something like, "Did you just ask me if you could pray for me— seriously?!! What Are You Thinking?!" Come on, you know you want to do this! Dude, please tell me that you are reading this: I've got to know! Following Jesus so that we can hear His voice seems pretty straightforward, but it is more complex than we realize because of our resistance to giving control of our lives to the Lord. Yet if we are serious about wanting to move into listening prayer, then we need to take surrender seriously. Obedience is hard because we don't like anybody telling us what to do. Even toddlers are adamant about what they want and what they don't want. But fighting through our resistance to obedience is worth it if we want to partner with Jesus and the Holy Spirit to move in to the adventures that the Lord has for us to walk out. Jesus said, "My sheep listen to my voice, I know them, and they follow me" (John 10:27). To be identified as His sheep, we must listen to His voice, and then we need to follow what He says. If we obey, the Holy Spirit lights us up with the light of Christ: "We are witnesses of these things, and so is the Holy Spirit, whom God has given to those who obey him" (Acts 5:32). So here is the challenge. We need to completely yield our will to the Lord's will. Often, we agree with this yielding in principle. After all, it sounds so good, and even so humble, to say you've yielded to God's will. But truly yielding our wants and desires is another thing entirely. As with everything that we are trying to do in listening prayer, Jesus is the one whom we need to look to first to help us get our hearts in the right place so that we will have ears to hear.

The obedience to the Father that Jesus walked in while He lived on earth is inspiring, to say the least. Philippians 2 tells us that Jesus laid His divinity down and lived as we do, except without sin. Let's look at this verse again: "And being found in appearance as a man, he humbled himself by becoming obedient to death—even death on a cross!" (Phil. 2:8). So, Jesus was obedient even to the point of having to die on the cross. Jesus was so committed to living in obedience that everything that He taught was just what the Father told Him to say. "[49] For I did not speak on my own, but the Father who sent me commanded me to say all that I have spoken. [50] I know that his command leads to eternal life. So whatever I say is just what the Father has told me to say" (John 12:49-50).

But Jesus doesn't stop here; He shows us that the way He

lived in total obedience is the best way for us to live, too. In the Great Commission, Jesus said that we are to do everything He has commanded:

> [18] ... All authority in heaven and on earth has been given to me. [19] Therefore go and make disciples of all nations, baptizing them in the name of the Father and of the Son and of the Holy Spirit, [20] and teaching them to obey everything I have commanded you. And surely I am with you always, to the very end of the age. (Matt. 28:18-20).

Listen to the instructions that Jesus left for His disciples on the way to live out our everyday lives: "... Whoever wants to be my disciple must deny themselves and take up their cross daily and follow me" (Luke 9:23). In other words, we must die to what we want and live for what the Lord wants. Such submission to the will of God the Father is absolutely foreign to the way that we think. Yet, we are called to have the same mindset Jesus had.

Errand, rerouted

Jared had an errand to do but he got in prayer to go to a bigger store much further away than the neighborhood store that would have been so much quicker. Jared obeyed, even though his mind argued with this directive from the Holy Spirit. When he finally got to the store, the tax booth he was looking for was closed. He asked a cashier who wasn't busy about it. They ended up striking up a conversation about the university emblazoned on Jared's sweatshirt because the cashier recognized the school. Jared realized that this lady was the reason he was sent to this store. He asked if he could pray for her before he left, and she said, "Yes, that would be great."

Jared shares the rest of story: "'I plead the blood of Jesus and command that only the Holy Spirit would come close and prosper,' I began. The prayer seemed generic to me. I remember praying against frustration towards family members and about God's goodness and faithfulness. When I finished praying, the woman looked at me with bleary eyes and said softly, 'You have no idea what this means to me. You have no idea what is going on in my family and yet....' She took a breath and paced a small circle: 'Wow, just wow.' I then proceeded to tell her how God had led me specifically to that store because of her, and He loved her to the point of sending someone to pray for her. I thought she was going to lose it right there in the walkway, but her coworker called her back over to her register. She gave me a brief hug, and thanked me again." Jared ran into her a few months later and she told him the backstory to the incredible prayer he had prayed for her. "She said that things had been much better since the prayer. So, I prayed for her again and encouraged her some more. God is so good!"

ﻋﻠﻰ

Listen to this admonition in which Jesus powerfully lays out abandoning ourselves to the will of God:

> 23 ... The hour has come for the Son of Man to be glorified. 24 Very truly I tell you, unless a kernel of wheat falls to the ground and dies, it remains only a single seed. But if it dies, it produces many seeds. 25 Anyone who loves their life will lose it, while anyone who hates their life in this world will keep it for eternal life. 26 Whoever serves me must follow me; and where I am, my servant also will be. My Father will honor the one who serves me. (John 12:23-26)

Obedience is a major theme of discipleship. Consider that Jesus' basic invitation to his disciples was to follow him. But what does following look like for us? Simply put, we are to obey His commands in the Word of God (Matt. 28:19) and we are to listen to His commands through the Holy Spirit (Rev. 3:19-22). A surrendered heart is essential to move and live in to listening prayer. But how do we deal with the serious resistance that we feel toward obeying Jesus like this? Everything in us screams "No! Freedom is doing what I want, not what God wants," or so we think.

The summer before the freshman year in college is a tremendous time of transition. Often, parents struggle the most. During the summer of 2016, I had the opportunity to pray for revival on a number of university campuses. As it so happened, it was Parent's Day on many of these campuses. I saw many students getting ready enter a brand-new life walking around with parents. For the students, there is excitement, fear, and a fervent desire to look older than they are. The facial expressions on their parents' faces can be poignant, and looks of anxiety and sadness often sneak up on parents during this intense time of letting go.

The first year in college is incredibly challenging. What in the world, as a student, do you do with all the new freedoms? Our culture defines freedom as doing whatever it is that you want to do. What happens to new college students? Many go after all kinds of forbidden fruit on their "adventure of a lifetime." Hey, it's the time of your life when you are supposed to do what you want, kind of like a perpetual Mardi Gras, right? But doing whatever our sinful nature wants to do is more like slavery than freedom, and the emptiness that follows is profound. Josh McDowell described it as the loneliest thrill you will ever know.

The loneliness and emptiness can reach almost unbearable levels. What finally occurs to you is that there has to be more to life than this. At the end of Solomon's life, despite experiencing every conceivable form of pleasure, he decided that living life following pleasure was meaningless and like chasing after the wind. For Solomon, in spite of experiencing the arts in all its fullness, having a harem, and having great wealth, his life had become pointless and empty (Eccles. 2:1-11). He came to the conclusion that the fear of the Lord is the beginning of wisdom. Here is the irony of all ironies: when we live in complete surrender to the Lord Jesus Christ, we finally experience true freedom. When we begin to live out the purpose and destiny that the Lord has for each of our lives, we experience joy unspeakable:

> [9] As the Father has loved me, so have I loved you. Now remain in my love. [10] If you keep my commands, you will remain in my love, just as I have kept my Father's commands and remain in his love. [11] I have told you this so that my joy may be in you and that your joy may be complete. (John 15:9-11)

One of Satan's favorite lies to college students (and the lie isn't limited to college students) is that you will have a boring life if you choose to follow Jesus. But I can tell you, when you make the decision to follow Jesus, and when you say yes to listening prayer, you will see boring in the rearview mirror. Our culture tries to convince college students to believe that they will experience heaven on earth doing whatever they want to do at spring break on the beach. College students flock to beaches during spring break, searching for the adventure of a lifetime. A number of us have had the privilege of sharing the gospel in word and deed at the beach during spring break. One of the acts of kindness that Christian groups do during spring break is to offer free van rides.

On one of these van rides at the beach, I shared with a student that the greatest adventure she could ever go on was to follow Jesus. After thinking about it, she said that she guessed she had never learned to do adventure the right way before. At a pancake breakfast one morning, I asked a table full of college students if I could pray for them. One of the girls volunteered right away. She was excited when I told her to read the book of Acts because her name was all over it. I said to her, "You are not afraid of anything, are you?" She said, "No, I'm really not." "The book of Acts is definitely for you. You have no idea the adventure that Jesus wants to make out of your life." She told me, "I have never read that before! I'll have to read it!"

Bill had invited me to go to Panama City Beach with his group that was going to give free van rides to spring breakers and witness to them about Jesus. Isn't it interesting that adventure tends to sound much better in theory rather than when you actually start to do it! Bill was there to greet me when I pulled up to the hotel where we were staying for the week. When we got on the elevator, I was immediately shoved right in to awkward. There Bill and I were, two older guys facing an elevator full of spring breakers who were ready to hit the beach. Bill loves to embrace the awkward, so he turned to one of the girls and said, "Did you call your mother today?" She said, "Yes," with some serious attitude. Then Bill said, "Because she is praying for you and your grandma." I turned to one of the guys and gave him a high five and said, "And we are two pastors." The whole elevator erupted into sound. They were still hollering when we got off the elevator and it was pulling away. I told Bill, "I think I'm going to stay close to you this week; that was hilarious!"

For the first two years at Panama City Beach, I had a "Free Prayer" sign on the beach and had incredible experiences helping students become surprised by God. There is no way to describe what it feels like to watch someone stagger off after receiving listening prayer because they have been profoundly touched by the Holy Spirit. Why do they stagger off? Typically, what happens is Jesus gives them a glimpse of who He has created them to become. Jesus called Simon *Peter*, or *Cephas*, which means rock. Simon was impulsive and he denied knowing Jesus out of fear right before Jesus was crucified. But Jesus didn't just see him for who he was when He originally called Simon to follow Him, but saw Simon for who he could become, and then called this out in Simon Peter. In listening prayer, Jesus calls people out of where they are and into the destiny and purpose for which they were created. Once we clearly see this destiny and calling that the Lord has for our lives, it suddenly makes sense to lay our sin down at the foot of the cross. Hopefully, like Simon

Peter, those that we pray for will say *yes* to Jesus as Savior and Lord and *yes* to the destiny and purpose for which Jesus created them:

> For we are His workmanship [His own master work, a work of art], created in Christ Jesus [reborn from above—spiritually transformed, renewed, ready to be used] for good works, which God prepared [for us] beforehand [taking paths which He set], so that we would walk in them [living the good life which He prearranged and made ready for us]. (Eph. 2:10 AMP)

Often after praying for spring breakers, I tell them that I love to pray for them because I know how much they love adventure. I then say that I'm just there to tell them that the greatest adventure they could ever go on is to follow Jesus. To a person, whenever I share this adventure message, they become strangely silent and go to a place deep in thought.

Jesus longs to make a miracle of your life for the sake of the Kingdom of God. Listen to what Jesus said that He could do with our lives if we will give Him control: "The thief enters only to steal, kill, and destroy. I came so that they could have life—indeed, so that they could live life to the fullest" (John 10:10 CEB). Jesus wants us to live life to its fullest! When we believe in Jesus as the Son of God and follow Him, we begin to walk out the very purpose that God created us for. This is the adventure that you and I were meant to walk out, and it's amazing beyond words when you discover it!

Listen to the incredible life that we are invited to live once we say to Jesus, "Come and take over. I've seen what I can do with my life Lord; I ask You to come in and do what only You can do, Jesus."

> 12-14 So don't you see that we don't owe this old do-it-yourself life one red cent. There's nothing in it for us, nothing at all. The best thing to do is give it a decent

burial and get on with your new life. God's Spirit beckons. There are things to do and places to go!

15-17 This resurrection life you received from God is not a timid, grave-tending life. It's adventurously expectant, greeting God with a childlike "What's next, Papa?" God's Spirit touches our spirits and confirms who we really are. We know who he is, and we know who we are: Father and children. And we know we are going to get what's coming to us—an unbelievable inheritance! We go through exactly what Christ goes through. If we go through the hard times with him, then we're certainly going to go through the good times with him! (Rom. 8:12-17 MSG)

Late one night in a van giving free rides to spring breakers, I said to a group of guys from Massachusetts, "You know what you guys are looking for? You are looking for adventure." Suddenly, I had their undivided attention. One of the guys asked me, "What do you do for fun?" I said, "Dude, it's 1:30 in the morning, I'm 61 years old, I'm in a van giving free rides to spring breakers, and I'm praying for you and telling you about Jesus; I think I'm having it right now!" Every night the same guys requested our van and I got to pray for them, over and over again. Jesus through the Holy Spirit was giving them a glimpse of who they could become should they say "Yes!" to the adventure Jesus was offering them. So, Massachusetts dudes: message me, you are in the book! So, how about it: are you ready to go on the adventure of a lifetime by following Jesus?

Listen to Shalisha's testimony from a time of outreach at the beach:

Free Prayer

"It was a few years ago, now, but I was just learning how to put listening prayer into practice. I was on location at Panama City Beach with an outreach to spring breakers. I

was there with my campus ministry group and with my good friend Pastor Tim Jones, affectionately known as PT in my circle of friends.

"We were taking our time down on the beach one afternoon, as we set up shop on the beach with a sign beaming FREE PRAYER. At this point it was a couple days into the week so I should have been exhausted on this particular afternoon; however, I felt an exciting amount of energy. The idea of praying for people was the only thing on my mind. The first couple of stops I made were good. There were groups of guys and girls all nicely sunburned by this point: some were accepting, others were taken aback, and still others were sincerely grateful.

"As the day went on many came and went but there was one stop I will never forget. They were highlighted to me, but I had to run to catch them. It was two early twenty-something guys. They were friendly and quickly said 'Sure' to my offer of prayer. The one being prayed for was wearing sunglasses, so I found it a bit hard to read how he was taking the prayer. As I prayed, the Holy Spirit spoke. He showed me a picture of the guy in a closed-off room playing video games. The Lord then filled my mouth, 'Thank you, Lord, that You are calling him out of fantasy, into reality, giving him a sword to do battle with in the real world.' He was frozen. His friend on the other hand was now quite animated; he said something like, 'Dude, No way! He is going into the army next month!' No more was the friend the only one animated. I might have geeked out a bit, too. I said something like, 'What!? Wow! Really?' I was so overcome with the reality of what just happened that I stepped back and said, 'Okay, well, you enjoy that. Jesus loves you. I am going to go fall on my face now.'

"I was so overcome with the joy of the Lord that I just laid there with my knees burning in the sand and my hands covering my face. 'How can I, a sophomore, have the *privilege of knowing the God of Heaven's heart for His creation?' At that point I was not thinking theology or doctrine, I was simply overcome with the love of a Father over his daughter as He whispered, 'Well done, my girl.'"*

I have become convinced that many fall into forbidden fruit because they have said *no* to the adventure that the Holy Spirit has for them. The intimacy and excitement that we long for are found when we say *yes* to Jesus at the deepest level of our beings. I like to ask students if they would rather ride a kiddie train ride or a ride like the Diamondback rollercoaster at King's Island. Almost all of them immediately choose the rollercoaster. My next question is why? They answer that it's more exciting. My next question is why is it more exciting? I keep asking questions like this until they admit that what makes a ride great is the element of fear. I then say, "So, in other words, if there were no fear, then it would be a boring ride." I close in to make my point: "So why is it that we do everything we can to take out all the fear in the Christian life? Why is it then that we get so offended if we are challenged to leave our comfort zone and take risks of faith for Jesus?" I share my favorite John Wayne quote at this point. "Courage is being scared to death but saddling up anyway."

Toward the end of 2016, I received in prayer to start a campus ministry outreach at Eastern Kentucky University. For about a month, I did some prayer drives on the campus. On one of those prayer drives, Travis spotted me while he was out walking and praying for his campus. He was on the phone with his fiancée, Bitty, and he said, "Hey that's PT driving by, I wonder if that is some kind of sign." A week later, Travis and I were meeting and making plans together to reach his campus. That's how the Lord works, and it's awesome!

So, turn the clock ahead, and Travis and I are now praying for student-athletes each week with listening prayer and are witnessing the love of Jesus being poured out into their hearts.

As Travis and I move around and pray for each student, the Holy Spirit's anointing is incredible as we listen in prayer. The first night that we did this, Travis said he felt like crying a number of times because the love of Jesus was so tangible and real. As I was leaving that first night, I told Travis that I had felt a little intimidated and nervous before the prayer time started. But I also told him I've learned that all I have to do is show up and the Lord will show up, too, without fail! That night the students were excited beyond words because of the way the Holy Spirit touched them with Jesus' love. We have continued to watch these student-athletes become more and more excited each week as they realize what an adventure it is to follow Jesus!

My hope is that somehow these stories are an encouragement for you to go on your own adventures with Jesus. I shared this "Go on Adventures with Jesus" message in a church in Arizona and was excited to learn that one of the men who was retired responded to the message by setting up a free prayer sign along the side of the road where he lives and he had some powerful experiences praying for people with listening prayer. Listening prayer is all about going on adventures with Jesus. Going on adventures is not just for young people or for people that minister to college students. The Lord has unique adventures for each one of us. But make no mistake about it: the adventure really begins when we fully surrender to Jesus' leadership in our lives.

Here is a short gospel message I share with students on spring break:

Can I share with you the good news about Jesus?

God loves us and created us to live close to his heart and to go on adventures with Him. (John 10:10)
But something went wrong: we decided to do what we wanted to do rather than what God wanted us to do. (Isa. 53:3-6)
So, God went to extreme lengths to win us back. God sent his beloved Son Jesus to the earth, but we

crucified Him, but then God raised Him from the dead to provide The Way for us to come home to Him. (John 14:6)

So, on behalf of Jesus:

Do you believe that Jesus is the Son of God? (John 3:16)

Yes, Jesus is my King.

Will you ask Jesus to forgive you of your sins? (Luke 24:46-47)

Yes, Jesus is my Savior.

Will you ask Jesus to be your leader?

Yes, Jesus is my Lord. (Rom. 10:9)

Will you say yes to Jesus?

Surrender prayer: *Dear Lord, I believe that Jesus is the Son of God and that You raised Him from the dead. Thank You for forgiving me of my sins because of Jesus dying for me. I ask Jesus to be my Savior and my Lord. I give myself completely to Jesus and surrender to His leadership in my life. Thank You for the gift of eternal life and for the privilege of living for Jesus for the rest of my life. In Jesus' name, I pray. Amen.*

As an act of obedience to Jesus, you will want to be baptized and become a part of a group of believers that have decided to follow Jesus.

Typically, people are good with the message until it gets to the point about surrendering to the Lord's leadership. The lie that Satan feeds students is very real, and they believe that if they say yes to Jesus right now they will miss out on fun and adventure and will always regret it. I have seen people struggle, get really quiet, and say something like, "I need some more time to think about this." I will never forget what an amazing young mother who is now living for Jesus told me: "I wish I had run into people like you guys when I was on the beach during spring break. It could have saved me so much heartache, pain, and disappointment."

Surrendering to Jesus' leadership in your life is the way to freedom. This statement seems like such a paradox. How can giving up your freedom possibly make you free? The seeming contradiction offends our minds and so we keep saying *no* to this offer from Jesus. Hopefully, we discover the truth about what real freedom is sooner rather than later. In the season right before I moved into learning to listen to the Lord in prayer, I had become very disillusioned with myself. I had the good sense to finally come to the conclusion that I was incompetent to run my life. So, I did the only thing that made any sense. I said to myself, "You have proven that you are incompetent to run my life so, you're fired!" On one occasion after sharing this in a message, I invited people forward to the altar rail to officially fire themselves and to ask to come under Jesus' management.

A couple of months later, I attended a men's retreat for this church and spoke on listening prayer. Afterwards, I got to pray for a number of the men. One of the guys that I prayed for told me that he was one of the ones that was there that night I preached and he had come down to the altar and fired himself. He had asked to come under Jesus' management and had told Jesus that he was ready for a new life. The next day when he got to work, he was fired. That wasn't the end of his story, though; it ends with good news. He was now working a job where he only made about half of what he made before, but he had never been happier.

There are many of us who only seem to be able to learn by running our heads into a brick wall. It is inspiring to see students who decide they are going to live all in with Jesus without having to go through the nonsense of chasing after the wind that is offered out in the world. Regardless of what stage of life you are in, it is never too late to surrender to Jesus' leadership. Many of us should have made this radical surrender a lot sooner than we actually did. Over the years, I have seen prodigal sons and daughters realize that what they need to do is to come home to the Lord. In the prodigal son story (Luke 15), there were really two prodigals. One left home and wasted his substance in wild living. The other stayed home, outwardly followed all the rules, but was prodigal in his heart. Many who go to church faithfully year after year don't even realize that they are prodigals in their hearts. They are living outside of the Lord's leadership for their lives and are miserable. Let's face it: as I stated at the beginning of this chapter, human beings do not like being told what to do. As I said earlier, if you don't believe this, try to work with preschoolers. You will see very quickly that a rebellious heart starts early in life.

So how about it, are you ready to lay rebellion down? Are you willing to do what should have been done a long time ago— are you willing to finally fire yourself? Jesus will do a much better job of being in charge of you than you will anyway! But here is the deal: His leadership is not boring. Jesus will take you well outside of your comfort zone. You will live life under a new normal. But your new normal will mean that you will have to step out of whatever box you have created. Then you can influence people for the sake of the Kingdom of God. Why put this off another moment? Life is just too short. Let's move into the destiny, purpose, and adventure that Jesus has for us!

> *Dear Lord, I lay my rebellion down and as of this day I fire myself. Jesus, You are in charge, and it is with joy that I am finally coming completely under Your management. I ask You, Jesus, to take me on whatever adventures are in Your heart for my life. In Jesus' name, I pray. Amen.*

CHAPTER 12

Teach Me to Pray, Jesus

The good news about doing whatever you want in life is that it doesn't work. Oh, it may work in the short run, but after a while we begin to think, "There has to be more to life than this. I am doing whatever I want and I am still empty." Once we receive the good news of the gospel of Jesus, we are introduced to a new way of living. The difference in our lives can be like night to day. Instead of avoiding all conversation about the Lord and seeing Him as an unwelcome intrusion, suddenly, we not only welcome the Lord's involvement, but we actually want Him to direct our lives. This chapter is for the person saying: "Yes, Lord, I really want Your will for my life, but how do I test the things that I am receiving in prayer? And how can I begin to listen in prayer about issues that are really close to my heart?"

When we first move into the practice of listening prayer, the process feels simple, yet amazing. We see Jesus pour out His love into others' hearts by using ordinary people like ourselves to join in with Jesus' prayers for them. As we begin to get confirmation that we really are hearing from the Lord by praying for others, we become more and more confident about hearing

Jesus' voice. We even begin to listen in prayer about the Lord's will for our own lives. However, we soon learn that the process of listening in prayer for ourselves is quite a bit more complex than listening in prayer for others. In fact, it can be confusing. Sometimes we get frustrated enough that we are even tempted to stop trying to listen to the Lord in prayer for His will for our lives. This is what Satan wants us to do. He hates it when we begin to partner with the Holy Spirit at a deep heart level, because believers that love both the Bible and partnering with the Holy Spirit are lethal to the kingdom of darkness. So, what do we do when confusion seems to camp out in our prayer lives?

The closer an issue is to our hearts, the more difficult it is to get our desires, fears, doubts, and pride out of the way so that we can hear from the Lord. Sometimes we get into an uncomfortable place where we are not sure if we are hearing the Lord's voice, our own thoughts, our desire to please others, or a lie that Satan is trying to slip in on us. Listen to what Paul had to say about the importance of testing what we believe God is saying to us:

> [19] Do not quench the Spirit. [20] Do not treat prophecies with contempt [21] but test them all; hold on to what is good, [22] reject every kind of evil. [23] May God himself, the God of peace, sanctify you through and through. May your whole spirit, soul and body be kept blameless at the coming of our Lord Jesus Christ.
>
> (1 Thess. 5:19-23)

One day I asked the Lord if there was one scripture passage to sum up what I had been learning about listening prayer. What I heard in my heart was the Lord's Prayer. Because the words of the Lord's Prayer are so familiar, we're sometimes likely to dismiss it with a wave of the hand: "Oh I know all that. I thought I was supposed to learn something that I don't already know." Yet as I began to study the Lord's Prayer, I was amazed at the depth of truth and all the gold in it, especially as it relates to listening prayer.

I was giving a group of college guys a hard time about their request to teach them to move into listening prayer. I told them, "I can teach you about it but it's not going to do any good." Next, I said, "If this was a group of college women, they would get it right away." (Imagine various non-verbal sounds of disapproval at this point.) "Oh, why am I saying this? If this was a group of college women, I would teach them how to move into this, and then they would actually do the things that I showed them to do. You guys, on the other hand, won't use what I give you. There are two things you are going to think when I try to teach you about this. First, you are going to think, 'It's not my idea—it can't be that great,' and then secondly you are going to think, 'I'm going to come up with a better way of doing this.'" Next, I asked them, "What is this?" They responded, "Pride???" I asked, "Have I beat you up enough?" They assured me that I had.

Matt broke the tension in the room and said, "PT, you gave me the Lord's Prayer to use a year ago and I still haven't used it!" Everyone laughed really hard as I gave Matt a fist pump and said, "That's what I'm talking about!" The next thing that happened was incredible. The guys said, "PT, seriously, teach us how to listen in prayer!" After we went through the teaching on the Lord's Prayer, everyone took a turn in the middle of the circle and we listened in prayer for that person. Guys who had never heard the Lord before in prayer suddenly started receiving. We were beyond excited about what was happening. Think about it, why wouldn't the key be the Lord's Prayer? When the disciples asked Jesus how to pray, this is what He taught them. So rather than saying, "Yeah, yeah, I know all that," why not listen to the Lord's Prayer with a different set of ears? What if there is so much more in the Lord's Prayer than we ever imagined?

As we pray through the Lord's Prayer, our hearts are put at rest. Praying through the Lord's Prayer helps us discern the leading of the Holy Spirit for issues close to our hearts. The Lord's Prayer ushers us into the presence of the Lord so that we can receive from Him and helps us learn how to stay in step with the Spirit. "Since we live by the Spirit, let us keep in step with the Spirit" (Gal. 5:25).

The Lord's Prayer moves us into the anointing of the Holy Spirit and the anointing of the Holy Spirit helps us know the truth. In fact, the Holy Spirit is often called the Holy Spirit of Truth: "But you have an anointing from the Holy One [you have been set apart, specially gifted and prepared by the Holy Spirit], and all of you know [the truth because He teaches us, illuminates our minds, and guards us from error]" (1 John 2:20 AMP).

But how do we know if we are moving in the anointing of the Holy Spirit after we've prayed through the Lord's Prayer? The most basic answer to this question is two-fold. First, Jesus is acknowledged as the Son of God:

> [1]Dear friends, do not believe every spirit, but test the spirits to see whether they are from God, because many false prophets have gone out into the world. [2] This is how you can recognize the Spirit of God: Every spirit that acknowledges that Jesus Christ has come in the flesh is from God, [3] but every spirit that does not acknowledge Jesus is not from God. This is the spirit of the antichrist, which you have heard is coming and even now is already in the world. (1 John 4:1-3)

Secondly, when we stay in step with the Spirit the way Paul talked about in Galatians 5, the fruit of the Holy Spirit will be evident. The anointing of the Holy Spirit happens when we experience the Holy Spirit's love, joy, peace, patience, kindness, goodness, faithfulness, gentleness, and self-control. I often ask people if frustration is on that list, and they say, "No." Then I say, "Too bad; I seem to be really good at frustration." When we are in a state of frustration, or fear, or anger, or hopelessness, or impatience, we are not ready to listen in prayer yet. So, how about it, are you ready to see how Jesus' model prayer will prepare you to receive the leadership of the Holy Spirit for your life?

Our Father, Who Art in Heaven

When Jesus prayed, heaven touched earth. His connection with the Father was obvious. You can understand then why the disciples asked Jesus to teach them to pray. Jesus started the model prayer with "Our Father, who art in heaven." The *our* in this phrase teaches that the personal relationship Jesus had with God the Father was available to all those who are Jesus' disciples. But for many people, starting out a prayer with *Our Father* is not good news. If a person's relationship with their earthly father is filled with pain, appealing to a father can seem impossible.

Ruth had an incredibly broken relationship with her dad. Her dad was violent and not the kind of person you would ever want to be close to. I asked Ruth, "Is it hard for you to pray 'Our Father'"? She said, "Not at all: God is the Father that I never had." Satan wants to lie to us about who God is. But Ruth knew the truth about God the Father: He is like Jesus. Listen:

> ⁶ Jesus answered, "I am the way and the truth and the life. No one comes to the Father except through me. ⁷ If you really know me, you will know my Father as well. From now on, you do know him and have seen him."
>
> ⁸ Philip said, "Lord, show us the Father and that will be enough for us."
>
> ⁹ Jesus answered: "Don't you know me, Philip, even after I have been among you such a long time? Anyone who has seen me has seen the Father. How can you say, 'Show us the Father?'" (John 14:6-9)

Jesus was invited to a religious leader's home and a woman from the street began to wash Jesus' feet with her tears and poured expensive perfume on his feet while Jesus was reclining at the table. Much to the surprise of the religious leaders around that table, Jesus told a story in which the woman was the hero of the story. Jesus contrasted the woman's lavish gift of hospitality and love for him with the lack of hospitality and love that Simon, the host of the meal, had shown to him. Jesus told the people around the table that the woman was forgiven much because she loved much (Luke 7:36-50). This story speaks to us about the extraordinary love of Jesus. Jesus loved the outcast and forgotten so much that He would place His hands on lepers, whom others treated as untouchable, to pray for their healing. Just think of it, when we look at Jesus, we see what God our Father looks like.

It is powerful to watch a small child run down a driveway with his or her arms wide open, ready to be caught up in a big hug by a parent or favorite relative who has come home. When we pray *Our Father*, we are invited to run down the driveway with our arms wide open to the Lord. Frank has a grandson that he has seen once a week for the past three years of his life, ever since his grandson was eighteen months old. His grandson runs to him with his arms wide open and jumps into Pa-Frank's arms when he arrives. One day as Frank was listening in prayer, the Lord spoke to his heart, "You know how much you love your grandson; I love you more." One of the incredible benefits of listening to God in prayer is hearing how much He loves us! Jesus gave us a parable about a prodigal son who had asked for his share of the family inheritance before the father died then proceeded to waste it in wild living. The prodigal son got so low that he decided to go home, hoping that somehow he could at least become a servant in his father's house. To the son's total surprise, the father ran to meet him, welcomed him back into the family as a son, and threw a huge party for him (Luke 15:11-32). Jesus is making this kind of relationship with God the Father available to us as we pray.

However, because of the rebellion we feel and the desire to

be our own god that is imprinted on our human nature, our natural tendency is to run away from the Lord rather than to turn toward the Lord. This desire to run away rather than to seek the Lord throws up a major roadblock in our hearts to being receptive to the leading of the Holy Spirit. Paul describes our natural orientation to the Lord very well:

> [10] As it is written:
>
>> "There is no one righteous, not even one;
>> [11] there is no one who understands;
>> there is no one who seeks God.
>> [12] All have turned away,
>> they have together become worthless;
>> there is no one who does good,
>> not even one." (Rom. 3:10-12)

Let's face it, ever since the Garden of Eden, we have been hiding from God and blaming others for the sin that is in our lives. To make matters worse, because of our pride, we are naturally drawn to wanting to be our own gods. When we try to be our own gods, we believe that we get to decide what is right and wrong and so we plunge into the darkness. After we have allowed darkness into our lives, we can even begin to fall in love with the darkness and will even cling to it even though it is destroying us. So, the thought of coming before God, who is the Father of lights (James 1:17), sounds like something that is best put off for another day. But if our desire is to move into listening prayer, then we need to confess that without what Jesus did for us on the cross, we are unable to seek a personal relationship with God.

Because of the holiness of God's character, everything in us wants to run away and hide from the Lord. We are like the children of Israel that told Moses to go talk to the Lord on their behalf and tell us what He said:

[18] When the people saw the thunder and lightning and heard the trumpet and saw the mountain in smoke, they trembled with fear. They stayed at a distance [19] and said to Moses, "Speak to us yourself and we will listen. But do not have God speak to us or we will die." [20] Moses said to the people, "Do not be afraid. God has come to test you, so that the fear of God will be with you to keep you from sinning."

[21] The people remained at a distance, while Moses approached the thick darkness where God was. (Exod. 20:18-21)

If we hope to draw close to our holy Lord, we will need to come before God through Jesus. Because of Jesus, we can come to know God the way that the prodigal son in Jesus' parable got to know the Father. But like the prodigal son, we need to come to our senses. We need to humble ourselves before the Lord and we desperately need the blood of Jesus to provide the way into the holiness of the Lord's presence (Hebrews 10:19-23). So, when we pray *Our Father*, we are being moved into the personal relationship that Jesus made possible for us. Why not agree with these two prayers that Jesus and Paul prayed for us and draw close to the heart of the Lord:

Now this is eternal life: that they know you, the only true God, and Jesus Christ, whom you have sent.

(John 17:3)

I keep asking that the God of our Lord Jesus Christ, the glorious Father, may give you the Spirit of wisdom and revelation, so that you may know him better.

(Eph. 1:17)

Hallowed be Thy Name

The next phrase in the Lord's Prayer, "Hallowed be thy name," gives us the opportunity to humble ourselves and honor the Lord. When we truly pray "Hallowed be thy Name" from the heart, our pride is decimated, we recognize how holy the Lord is, and we give respect and honor to the Lord. The holiness of God changes us and prepares us to serve Him. When the Lord called Isaiah, Isaiah had an experience in the temple and was forever changed by the holiness of God's presence:

> [1] In the year that King Uzziah died, I saw the Lord, high and exalted, seated on a throne; and the train of his robe filled the temple. [2] Above him were seraphim, each with six wings: With two wings they covered their faces, with two they covered their feet, and with two they were flying. [3] And they were calling to one another:
>
> > "Holy, holy, holy is the LORD Almighty;
> > the whole earth is full of his glory."
>
> [4] At the sound of their voices the doorposts and thresholds shook and the temple was filled with smoke.
>
> [5] "Woe to me!" I cried. "I am ruined! For I am a man of unclean lips, and I live among a people of unclean lips, and my eyes have seen the King, the LORD Almighty."
>
> [6] Then one of the seraphim flew to me with a live coal in his hand, which he had taken with tongs from the altar. [7] With it he touched my mouth and said, "See, this has touched your lips; your guilt is taken away and your sin atoned for."
>
> [8] Then I heard the voice of the Lord saying, "Whom shall I send? And who will go for us?"

And I said, "Here am I. Send me!" (Isa. 6:1-8).

Isaiah got a glimpse of the righteousness and holiness of God and suddenly he was able to see his desperate need for atonement. As we come out of hiding and expose our hearts to the Lord in listening prayer, it is quickly apparent that we need to lay our pride down at the feet of Jesus. Everything in us resists this process. We hang on to our pride as if it were a life preserver. However, somehow, even though we don't like it, we know that our pride has to go if we are to move into the holiness of God's presence and into our Kingdom of God assignments. Listen to this admonition from the Lord:

> 10 See, I have refined you, though not as silver;
>   I have tested you in the furnace of affliction.
> 11 For my own sake, for my own sake, I do this.
>   How can I let myself be defamed
>   I will not yield my glory to another. (Isa. 48:10-11)

Jesus' ministry was a threat to the religious establishment of his day. There was a high cost to being identified with Jesus. Listen to this rebuke that Jesus spoke to a group of religious leaders:

> 36 I have testimony weightier than that of John. For the works that the Father has given me to finish—the very works that I am doing—testify that the Father has sent me. 37 And the Father who sent me has himself testified concerning me. You have never heard his voice nor seen his form, 38 nor does his word dwell in you, for you do not believe the one he sent. 39 You study the Scriptures diligently because you think that in them you have eternal life. These are the very Scriptures that testify about me, 40 yet you refuse to come to me to have life.
>
> 41 I do not accept glory from human beings, 42 but I know you. I know that you do not have the love of God in your hearts. 43 I have come in my Father's name, and

you do not accept me; but if someone else comes in his own name, you will accept him. [44] How can you believe since you accept glory from one another but do not seek the glory that comes from the only God?

(John 5:36-44)

These leaders couldn't hear the voice of God, so they couldn't rightly interpret scriptures. They did not have the love of God in their hearts and they sought their own glory rather than seeking to bring glory to the Lord. When we are ambitious for title and position and we care a great deal about being admired by people, our hearts can shut down to being able to hear from the Lord in prayer.

Human beings get really soul-sick when we try to receive glory for ourselves that should only be given to the Lord. Because of the Lord's great love for us, we often need to be refined in the fire. The Lord disciplines those He loves. We don't like this message. We recoil from the thought of having to have our character refined by the Lord. The Lord wants to use us for His Kingdom in profound ways, but in order to do this, He often needs to conform us to be more like Christ.

I love sports as well as many of you. But there is a huge temptation in sports: it's the desire to go after personal glory. For those of you who are athletes, you can attest to the temptation to go after glory. Even fans can get swept up in the temptation. How we feel about ourselves can be profoundly impacted by whether our team wins or loses. Fans can begin to live vicariously through a famous sports star and can become hungry to share the experience of that star's glory. But, human beings do not do well when the motivation of their hearts is to go after personal glory. My favorite athletes are the ones who use their sport as a platform to be a witness for Jesus. We are hardwired to do something of significance with our lives. This desire for greatness is incredible when it is used the right way—making Jesus' name great with our lives purifies and fulfills this desire for greatness.

When we pray, "Hallowed be thy name," we are sanctifying our hearts to make Jesus and God the Father's name great rather than our own. After all, some day we will face the Lord and our work for the Lord will be tested with fire. Every motivation of our heart will be exposed. The supposed work that we did for the Lord that was motivated by pride or the desire to make a name for ourselves will be burned up:

> 11 For no one can lay any foundation other than the one already laid, which is Jesus Christ. 12 If anyone builds on this foundation using gold, silver, costly stones, wood, hay or straw, 13 their work will be shown for what it is, because the Day will bring it to light. It will be revealed with fire, and the fire will test the quality of each person's work. 14 If what has been built survives, the builder will receive a reward. 15 If it is burned up, the builder will suffer loss but yet will be saved—even though only as one escaping through the flames. (1 Cor. 3:11-15)

Aaron and Miriam, Moses' brother and sister, spoke against Moses. "'Has the LORD spoken only through Moses?' they asked. 'Hasn't he also spoken through us?'" (Num. 12:2). In a statement laden with pride, not only did they speak against Moses, but they also thought that since God was speaking to Moses, surely He would speak to them in the same way. After all, Moses was their brother. What they were doing was challenging Moses' authority and calling from the Lord. Their pride blinded them to seeing that Moses was only doing what the Lord had told him to do. They, however, on their own apart from the leadership of the Lord, were deciding what their callings were. I suspect that they were blinded by their pride and failed to see that desiring prestige and status before people was motivating them. To drive the point home, right after Miriam and Aaron spoke against him, Moses is referred to as the most humble man on the face of the earth. Aaron and Miriam's pride was dealt with swiftly and severely

(Num. 12:10-14).

Saul was chosen by the Lord to be King. In the beginning, Saul was not impressed with himself and felt unworthy of the call of God. Early on, the Spirit of the Lord came upon Saul enabling him to hear the Lord's voice. But something happened to Saul: his pride took over. Not only did he not obey the Lord's instructions but he also acted as if he had done something of great religious significance by saying that he had spared the best of the animals for sacrifice when Samuel confronted him. You can see what was going on in Saul's heart when Saul goes and sets up a monument in his own honor: "Early in the morning Samuel got up and went to meet Saul, but he was told, 'Saul has gone to Carmel. There he has set up a monument in his own honor and has turned and gone on down to Gilgal'" (1 Sam. 15:12).

If this weren't bad enough, Saul tries to act as if his self-memorializing came from a pure heart:

> [13] When Samuel reached him, Saul said, "The LORD bless you! I have carried out the LORD's instructions."
>
> [14] But Samuel said, "What then is this bleating of sheep in my ears? What is this lowing of cattle that I hear?"
>
> [15] Saul answered, "The soldiers brought them from the Amalekites; they spared the best of the sheep and cattle to sacrifice to the LORD your God, but we totally destroyed the rest." (1 Sam. 15:13-15)

After a lot of back and forth with Samuel, Saul finally admitted his true motivations. The Lord dealt severely with Saul's pride. Stories like these in the Bible serve as a warning about the destructiveness of pride. An admonition from the Apostle Paul shows the importance of doing regular heart checks with the Lord: "[5] Examine yourselves to see whether you are in the faith; test yourselves. Do you not realize that Christ Jesus is in you—unless, of course, you fail the test?" (2 Cor. 13:5).

If we are serious about discerning the Lord's will for our lives, our hearts need to be fixed on bringing honor to the Lord rather than to ourselves. We are incredibly susceptible to pride, and so we need to check the condition of our heart with the Lord on a regular basis.

Besides personal glory, there is another side of pride that gets in the way of being able to receive from the Lord. As I said in Chapter 10, From Fear to Faith, this form of pride is fear-based. In this form of pride, our desire to please people and get their approval blocks our hearts to what the Lord wants to say. We can elevate pleasing people above pleasing God. Our ability to accurately discern the Lord's will is often negatively impacted by our desire to please the people who are close to us. Sometimes the Lord will give us something to do that cuts against the grain of what others think to help us to fall more in love with Him. The fear of what others think is crippling.

We need to learn about a different type of fear. This fear is a holy fear referred to in scripture as the fear of the Lord. This godly fear partners with the work of the Spirit. The example of the early disciples moving from behind locked doors into hostile public places to give witness to Jesus is testimony to the power of the Holy Spirit partnering with godly fear.

Listen to Isaiah's description of how the Spirit would be at work in Messiah Jesus:

> 2 The Spirit of the LORD will rest on him—
> the Spirit of wisdom and of understanding,
> the Spirit of counsel and of might,
> the Spirit of the knowledge and fear of the LORD—
> 3 and he will delight in the fear of the LORD. (Isa. 11:2-3a)

We typically don't think of the fear of the Lord, or treating God with the utmost honor or respect, as something to delight in. But when we learn to delight in the fear of the Lord, it helps us accurately discern what we are receiving in prayer as we partner with the Spirit. Once pleasing God becomes more important in our hearts than pleasing people, we have positioned ourselves to being open to whatever the Lord wants to say to us. When we pray, "Hallowed be thy Name," we get to lay down our desire for personal glory and our fears about what other people think about us. Why don't we let these verses move us into truly praying "Hallowed be thy Name" from the heart: "28 Therefore, since we are receiving a kingdom which cannot be shaken, let us have grace, by which we may serve God acceptably with reverence and godly fear. 29 For our God *is* a consuming fire" (Heb. 12:28-29). Then from the heart, we can truly say, "Holy, holy, holy is the Lord."

Thy Kingdom Come, Thy Will be Done on Earth as It is in Heaven

The next part of Jesus' model prayer is "Thy Kingdom come, thy will be done on earth as it is in heaven."

In 1995, I had the privilege of hearing Dr. Bill Bright, the founder of Campus Crusade for Christ, speak to a small group of people. He had recently spent a weekend fasting and praying with pastors and ministry leaders. Out of this experience, he wrote a book on revival and was looking for people who would fast for forty days for our nation. The passion and fire that poured out from his life as he spoke profoundly impacted me. I went up to speak to him and the peace and joy that radiated from his face literally lit up this 73-year-old. I said to myself, he knows something that I don't know. I started reading some of his books and stumbled across the little booklet "Have You Made the Wonderful Discovery of the Spirit-Filled Life?" After reading it, I said out loud, "Well, that is what's wrong with me. Christ is in my life but self is on the throne of my heart, and I need to be filled with the Holy Spirit."

Shortly after my encounter with Dr. Bright, I attended a Promise Keepers' gathering for clergy members in Atlanta. I had always had an extreme prejudice against raising hands in worship. Jack Hayford explained to the stadium of pastors that hands up is the universal sign of surrender around the world. Suddenly, raising hands in worship made more sense to me. Later, during worship, I heard these words in my heart, "Will you raise your hands to me?" At the time, I was clueless that the Lord was speaking to me. I said on the inside, "But Lord, if I raise my hands, the pastors I am with will think that I'm charismatic." Nevertheless, although very reluctantly, I raised my hands. To my total surprise there was an explosion in my heart and I said out loud, "So this is what worship is."

Everything in us resists living for God's purposes and plans for our lives. We want what we want, when we want it. If God's plans fit somehow into our plans, our dreams, or our goals, well then all is well and good. However, if the Lord wants us to do something that we don't want to do, forget it. Doesn't sound very good, does it? Yet, this attitude is deeply embedded in our hearts and goes all the way back to Adam and Eve.

The agony of Jesus in the Garden of Gethsemane is beyond our comprehension. As Jesus faced the reality of the pain and degradation that he was about to go through, he prayed: "...My Father, if it is not possible for this cup to be taken away unless I drink it, may your will be done" (Matt. 26:42).

Thankfully, Jesus went before us to show us the way. The game plan is simple—fix our eyes on Jesus and follow Him with a surrendered heart:

> ¹Therefore, since we are surrounded by such a great cloud of witnesses, let us throw off everything that hinders and the sin that so easily entangles. And let us run with perseverance the race marked out for us, ² fixing our eyes on Jesus, the pioneer and perfecter of faith. For the joy set before him he endured the cross, scorning its shame, and sat down at the right hand of the throne of God. ³ Consider him who endured such opposition from sinners, so that you will not grow weary and lose heart. (Heb. 12:1-3)

Give Us This Day Our Daily Bread

The next part of the model prayer that Jesus taught is "Give us this day our daily bread." This is a reminder of how God supernaturally provided manna in the wilderness for the children of Israel:

> 4 Then the LORD said to Moses, "I will rain down bread from heaven for you. The people are to go out each day and gather enough for that day. In this way I will test them and see whether they will follow my instructions. 5 On the sixth day they are to prepare what they bring in, and that is to be twice as much as they gather on the other days." (Exod. 16:4-5)

In spite of all the miracles God has done, people still ask, "Yes, but what have you done for me lately?" We are afraid that if we radically obey God, we won't have enough. Fear is a stumbling block to hearing the Lord's voice. Listen to Jesus' teaching from the Sermon on the Mount:

> 25 Therefore I tell you, do not worry about your life, what you will eat or drink; or about your body, what you will wear. Is not life more than food, and the body more than clothes? 26 Look at the birds of the air; they do not sow or reap or store away in barns, and yet your heavenly Father feeds them. Are you not much more valuable than they? 27 Can any one of you by worrying add a single hour to your life?
>
> 28 And why do you worry about clothes? See how the flowers of the field grow. They do not labor or spin. 29 Yet I tell you that not even Solomon in all his splendor was dressed like one of these. 30 If that is how God clothes the grass of the field, which is here today and tomorrow is thrown into the fire, will he not much more clothe you—you of little faith? 31 So do not worry,

saying, 'What shall we eat?' or 'What shall we drink?' or 'What shall we wear?' [32] For the pagans run after all these things, and your heavenly Father knows that you need them. [33] But seek first his kingdom and his righteousness, and all these things will be given to you as well. [34] Therefore do not worry about tomorrow, for tomorrow will worry about itself. Each day has enough trouble of its own. (Matt. 6:25-34)

This is a promise that Jesus is telling us that we need to believe. When we allow fear to come in and take over, then we believe that we are the source of our security rather than the Lord. Yet Jesus tells us when we seek His kingdom first we will have what we need. Sometimes we have to come to the end of our ability so that we will cry out to the Lord for His ability. If playing it safe takes over, we will say *no* to the risks of faith. When we allow fear to dominate our minds and our hearts, faith can seem inaccessible and it becomes difficult to hear from the Lord in prayer. Like Job, this is where we need to tell the Lord that we trust Him with our lives even though we don't understand. This is a promise from Jesus that we need to believe with all of our hearts so that we can clearly hear from Him: "Peace I leave with you; my peace I give you. I do not give to you as the world gives. Do not let your hearts be troubled and do not be afraid" (John 14:27).

Listen to this story that Pastor Paul shared in his own words:

Mixed emotions

"I have many stories to share especially about listening prayer but this story is something I am living through every day. Pastor Tim and I have had a relationship (ministry and mentor, friendship) for ten years. I have repeatedly asked him to come and minister to our students at every conference and retreat. We've done over twenty in the last ten years together. It was at one of those conferences that he prayed for my wife and me.

"Like he always does, he started by saying 'I plead the blood of Jesus....' Then he started to encourage us and helped us to dream about how much God had in store for our lives. Up to that point, it was a good prayer and one that we got completely excited about. Then, Pastor Tim said as he was listening to the Lord, 'God is moving you and you will go through a time of transitioning.' I believe his exact words were: 'Thank You, Lord, You are moving Paul and Eunha to the Pacific Northwest.' Now usually he is never that specific but I have known Pastor Tim long enough that I know he only shares what he hears.

"After he finished with his prayer, I had mixed emotions. I had finally felt at home in Dallas, Texas and we had a wonderful ministry for the last five years. My kids loved it, my wife loved it, and most of all, I was comfortable. A few months later he prayed again, and he again said, 'Thank You, Lord, that You are moving Paul and Eunha and that they will be moving to Seattle.' Now it wasn't just a region but a city. Needless to say, I didn't like that prayer and half-jokingly as Pastor Tim prayed for me, I said, 'Pastor Tim, I don't want you to pray for us anymore.'

"Now fast forward to where our family is situated. We have been in Seattle for over two years. God has been doing amazing things with the ministry I am part of, with our family, and with our children. Listening prayer is still something I wrestle with but I do know God loves to communicate with His children. I just want to be humble, hungry and willing to obey as we listen to Him."

ﷺ

Pastor Paul, after hearing this prayer, did what we should do with such prayers. Pastor Paul and Eunha began to seek the Lord to see if He would confirm this prayer in their own hearts. After they received confirmation in prayer, they began to see what it might look like and to pray about the possibility of doing ministry in Seattle. It was at least another year before anything took place. Finally, in the Lord's timing, the Lord provided the way for them to walk into this assignment from Him.

Forgive Us Our Trespasses as We Forgive Those Who Trespass Against Us

The next part of Jesus' model prayer is "Forgive us our trespasses as we forgive those who trespass against us." Unconfessed sin or bitterness in our hearts can get us completely off track with the Holy Spirit. Just as in the Garden of Eden, we are quick to hide from the Lord when we sin. And when we are confronted about our sin, we are quick to blame someone else rather than own what we have done. Since denial of our sin and self-justification runs so deep, we need the help of the Holy Spirit to show us the truth about our situation. Thankfully, the Holy Spirit is good at uncovering the truth:

> [7] But very truly I tell you, it is for your good that I am going away. Unless I go away, the Advocate will not come to you; but if I go, I will send him to you. [8] When he comes, he will prove the world to be in the wrong about sin and righteousness and judgment: [9] about sin, because people do not believe in me; [10] about righteousness, because I am going to the Father, where you can see me no longer; [11] and about judgment, because the prince of this world now stands condemned. (John 16:7-11)

We typically run away from the Lord like the Prodigal Son (Luke 15). But thankfully, the Holy Spirit is there to help us, and when we come to our senses, we need to come home to the Lord. At the Brownsville revival, many of us ran to the front of the room to repent and to make things right with the Lord. Everything in you will resist repenting. Your pride will scream at you to ignore conviction and justify your sin. But when Nathan the prophet confronted King David about his sin, David did the right thing and repented before God. At this point in Jesus' model prayer, we ask the Holy Spirit to expose everything that we need to repent of before God. After we repent, and place sin under the blood of Jesus, we will want to ask the Lord to address the potential bitterness that may be in our hearts.

After Jesus taught His disciples the Lord's Prayer, He immediately taught: "[14] For if you forgive other people when they sin against you, your heavenly Father will also forgive you. [15] But if you do not forgive others their sins, your Father will not forgive your sins" (Matt. 6:14-15).

Bitterness wreaks havoc on our ability to receive the Lord's leadership in prayer. It literally blocks our hearts from receiving from the Lord in prayer. If we try to listen to the Lord and we are offended when we are trying to listen, our offended, bitter, unforgiving attitude can make a mess. When we repent of our sin and forgive others that have offended us, the Holy Spirit gives the gift of peace and freedom. Where the Spirit of the Lord is, there is liberty!

On a prayer drive one day, I ended up at a church where I knew the pastor. Tammy was there and I had the privilege of praying for her. What I didn't know was that every time she came back to the church after that, she would check the parking lot to make sure that I wasn't there before she got out of her car. One day she had checked the parking lot to make sure I wasn't there and proceeded to get out of her car. In the Lord's perfect timing, I pulled up next to her and hopped out of my car before she could run away. Once again, she got prayed for. Sometime later she was walking into a coffee shop and complaining to a friend, "This random pastor keeps showing up and praying for me and it is freaking me out." Just as she said this, she looked over and said, "You can't be serious—there he is!" I wrote a prayer out on a card, walked up to her, gave it to her, and headed out. Tammy said the Lord had been dealing with her about some heart issues, which was why she was nervous about all this Holy Spirit listening prayer stuff. Let's be real, all of us have heart issues at one time or another. All of us need the cross of Jesus. As we move into the holiness of God's presence through the blood of Jesus through repentance of our sins and forgiving others, we are set free to hear from the Lord's heart for our lives. And yes, Tammy moved into listening prayer and her life has now impacted so many people. (You know you want to do this too!)

Lead Us Not into Temptation but Deliver Us from Evil

The next part of Jesus' model prayer that we need to pray through is "Lead us not into temptation, but deliver us from evil." Paul's comments from his first letter to the Corinthians sound like a commentary of this part of the Lord's Prayer:

> The only temptation that has come to you is that which everyone has. But you can trust God, who will not permit you to be tempted more than you can stand. But when you are tempted, he will also give you a way to escape so that you will be able to stand it.
>
> (1 Cor. 10:13 NCV)

The Lord has provided a way of escape for us when temptation from the enemy's camp tries to derail our calling from the Lord. When we pray this part of the prayer, we affirm the victory that is ours in the name of Jesus. When Jesus sent out his disciples during his earthly ministry, He gave them authority over evil spirits through the use of His name:

> [17] The seventy-two returned with joy and said, "Lord, even the demons submit to us in your name."
>
> [18] He replied, "I saw Satan fall like lightning from heaven. [19] I have given you authority to trample on snakes and scorpions and to overcome all the power of the enemy; nothing will harm you. [20] However, do

not rejoice that the spirits submit to you, but rejoice that your names are written in heaven."
(Luke 10:17-20)

The disciples knew through their ministry experiences that when Jesus taught them to pray "to deliver them from evil" that this victory was incredibly real. But it was after the cross that the words of this prayer became even more meaningful, not only for them, but also for us: "15 And having disarmed the powers and authorities, he made a public spectacle of them, triumphing over them by the cross" (Col. 2:15).

When we plead the blood of Jesus over times of listening prayer and when we come before the Lord in the name of Jesus, we defeat the attempts of the enemy's camp to stop what the Lord is doing through our lives. We also come against lies and deceit from the enemy's camp through this part of the Lord's Prayer. It can be difficult to hear from the Lord in spiritually dark areas because of interference from the forces of evil. Thankfully, when we plead the blood of Jesus over our time of prayer, we open the way for hearing from the Lord.

For Thine is the Kingdom, the Power, and the Glory

The last phrase from the Lord's Prayer is "For thine is the kingdom, the power, and the glory." At this point we join with heaven in worship of the Lamb:

> 11 Then I looked and heard the voice of many angels, numbering thousands upon thousands, and ten thousand times ten thousand. They encircled the throne and the living creatures and the elders. 12 In a loud voice they were saying:
>
> > "Worthy is the Lamb, who was slain,
> > to receive power and wealth and wisdom and
> > strength and honor and glory and praise!"

¹³ Then I heard every creature in heaven and on earth and under the earth and on the sea, and all that is in them, saying:

> "To him who sits on the throne and to the Lamb
> be praise and honor and glory and power,
> for ever and ever!"

¹⁴ The four living creatures said, "Amen," and the elders fell down and worshipped. (Rev. 5:11-14)

When we worship Jesus and tell Him how much we love Him, our hearts are set free to hear His voice!

Hey, why not go for it? You know you were born to do this! Say *yes* to listening prayer. "My sheep listen to my voice, I know them, and they follow me." Be an extreme sheep who listens to Jesus' voice and follows Him. Dare to listen to Him. He loves you: He really does! You know you were born for adventure. I'm just here to tell you that the greatest adventure you could ever go on is to follow Jesus!

Recommended Reading and References

Anderson, Neil T. 2006. *The Bondage Breaker.* Eugene, OR: Harvest House Publishers.

Blackaby, Henry, Richard Blackaby, and Claude King. 2008. *Experiencing God: Knowing and Doing the Will of God.* Nashville, TN: B&H Books.

Bright, Bill. 2008. *Have You Made the Wonderful Discovery of the Spirit-Filled Life?* Peachtree City, GA: New Life Resources.

Deere, Jack S. 1993. *Surprised by the Power of the Spirit: Discovering How God Speaks and Heals Today.* Grand Rapids, MI: Zondervan.

Kastner, Harold H. Jr. 1996. *In His Service.* Tallahassee, Fl.

Kraft, Charles H. 2010. *Two Hours to Freedom: A Simple and Effective Model for Healing and Deliverance.* Grand Rapids, MI: Chosen Books.

Weatherhead, Leslie D. 1929. *The Transforming Friendship: A Book About Jesus and Ourselves.* Nashville: Abingdon-Cokesbury Press.

Experience Listening Prayer Yourself and Share the Experience with Others!

~❦~

Pastor Tim loves to spread the word about Jesus' love through listening prayer, and welcomes invitations to speak at college campuses, youth group, and church events.

Find out more about the Experiencing Listening Prayer and Campus Thirst ministries through devotions and videos, and find details about hosting an Experiencing Listening Prayer weekend at **campusthirst.org** or email **PastorTim@campusthirst.org** for more information.